Financial Management in the 1990s

by

David Rawlinson and Brian Tanner

D1808548

General Editors: Michael Clarke and John Stewart

Longman

in association with the Local Government Training Board

Published by Longman Industry and Public Service
Management, Longman Group (UK) Ltd, 6th Floor, Westgate
House, The High, Harlow, Essex CM20 1YR, UK.

Telephone Harlow (0279) 442601
Fax (0279) 444501

First published 1990

British Library Cataloguing in Publication Data
Tanner, Brian
  Financial management in the 1990s. – (Managing local
  government).
  1. Great Britain. Local government. Financial management
  I. Title II. Rawlinson, David III. Series
  352.1'0941

ISBN 0-582-05622-5

ISBN 0-582-05622-5

Typeset by Communitype Communications Ltd
Printed and bound by Bell and Bain Ltd., Glasgow

Contents

Editors' Foreword

This book is one of the first in a new management series launched by the *Local Government Training Board* to be published by *Longman Group UK Ltd*. The series is designed to help those concerned with management in local government to meet the challenges of the next few years. It is based on the belief that in no period has it been so important for local authorities to have effective management.

The impact of government legislation is clear. Each local authority has to review its management, if it is to achieve an effective response. But the challenge is much deeper. In a changing society, new problems and issues demand from local authorities a capacity to respond in new ways. Local authorities have to become closer to their public as customer and citizen; resources have to be managed to achieve value in service; the requirement on all authorities is to achieve effective management of the changes which are taking place.

Effective management requires effective management development. The series is designed to aid the management development of present and future officers — and councillors. It is designed to be *used* by the reader in a variety of situations. While we hope that the books will be used on local government management courses we hope that they will have a much wider use.

They can be used by individuals or groups of managers or as the basis of seminars within authorities. However, the series will truly be a success if it becomes regarded as resource material for use in the business of management itself. We hope that the ideas discussed and the experience pooled will be a stimulus to more effective management.

The series is based on two principles. The first is the need for even greater emphasis on developing effective management in local government and the constant search for improvement. The second is that effective management must take account of the nature of local government. Need for effective management has already been stressed: the case for a separate series particular to local government is based on our second principle.

There are plenty of management books. What we have set out to produce is a series geared to the particular needs of local government. We would want to argue that those concerned with management in local government should draw on as wide a range of general experience as possible. Furthermore we would also want to agree that proper account is taken of the special purposes, conditions and tasks of local government. These books will help the manager to do just that. In publishing them we are not pretending that there is *one right way* to manage a local authority. Rather, we are exposing ideas and questions to help fashion the most helpful and effective approach to the local situation.

The first books in the sequence serve both to introduce the series and to highlight some of the key issues facing management in local authorities. The series will be extended by covering other issues of comtemporary concern which require to be tackled if management — and the health of the local authority — is to be improved.

Michael Clarke, Director, Local Government Training Board
Professor John Stewart, Institute of Local Government Studies

Dedication

This book is dedicated to our colleagues in the Treasurer's Department of Somerset County Council. We gratefully acknowledge their support during its preparation, and their stamina and resilience during the Management Team's campaign to put into practice the ideas set out in the following pages.

Introduction

Our objectives

The initial brief we were given was to write a book about financial management to be aimed specifically at non-finance managers. In other words it was intended to be a layman's guide to financial management as currently practised in local authorities.

On reflection we considered that both the value and the lifespan of such a book would be limited because changes of a fundamental nature are currently taking place in the local authority financial world. These changes relate both to:

▽   the nature of the finance function itself and;
▽   the environment governing all those people who are involved in delivering the final service — including particularly those who would at present describe themselves as non-finance managers.

Consequently we have decided to pursue twin objectives. As instructed we shall endeavour to explain the role, functions and techniques of financial management in a way which will be helpful to non-finance managers. We shall therefore minimise our use of financial jargon. Inevitably it has proved impossible to eliminate jargon altogether so we have appended a glossary of financial terms. This contains terms that we have used plus some others which non-finance managers may well have to contend with. What we have assumed is a reasonable knowledge of the structure and functions of local government. Although we have used English local government as our model, those more familiar with the Scottish and Welsh systems will not be at any significant disadvantage.

Readers whose immediate or only objective is to discover what financial management is about should read chapters 1 and 8 in full before using the summary sections at the start of the other chapters to identify issues of special interest.

Our second objective has been to 'gaze into the crystal ball'. In this book we shall put forward a view of financial management in local government which we feel will be in tune with the requirements of the 1990s. This is very much our vision and we are conscious that not only will there be many variations on the theme given here but also the theme itself has not yet found general acceptability. The conclusions in this book are not based on well-documented case histories. Dissenters could therefore argue that there is a lack of practical evidence to support some of our suggestions. However, there seems little doubt that at least some of the more novel concepts described here, such as core functions, minimum requirements and service level agreements, will become commonplace during the next ten years and indeed are becoming increasingly so as we write.

Those with financial management expertise who wish either to cast doubt on our vision or to benefit from our mistakes should concentrate on chapters 2, 9 and 10, and could well omit chapters 6, 7 and 8 altogether.

Finally by way of introduction we wish to stress that this book is not intended to be theoretical or academic. Neither is it intended to be a comprehensive text book on financial management. We have not even sought support for our views in existing published material and have not therefore provided a bibliography. This is a practical account of financial management in local government and a practitioner's view about where a process of change might lead. It is intended:

▽   to help non-finance managers to understand the financial management processes within local government; and
▽   to give them and others a wider perspective of the developments in financial management which will be necessary in the future, and their role in those developments.

The background

The world of local government has been with us for more than a century. Indeed it is the Association of County Councils (ACC) centenary this year. In the world of financial management we have reached possibly the most significant watershed of the entire period. The last thirty years have brought major changes in the structure, functions and financing of local government. Clearly these have had a profound effect on the way local authorities operate. However, financial management procedures have remained remarkably stable during this period; a strong central finance department has been the norm throughout and has been held to be one of the strengths of local government in terms of probity and accountability.

Developments in information technology initially encouraged this centralised approach, but more recently have provided increasing scope for decentralisation. Reinforcing this has been a growing emphasis on training and development; as a result more and more service managers are acquiring financial management skills. Consequently, variations on the theme of the strong central finance function are already established in many local authorities — just as they are in the private sector.

Now, however, we have a series of very major developments which offer a huge challenge to the financial management process in local authorities. These include:

▽   the advent of the community charge (or poll tax) from 1 April 1990 (see Appendix B);
▽   the new capital control arrangements which will apply from the same date (see Appendix C);
▽   the competitive tendering provisions of the Local Government Act 1988 which require a more commercial approach to the running of certain

services and a reliable and up to date financial management information system (see chapter 4);
▽   the growing requirement for decision making and accountability at the level of the individual establishment; the best examples are the provisions in the Education Reform Act 1988 for local management of schools and further education colleges;
▽   the possibility of wholesale transfers of local authority housing stock to the private sector under the tenants' choice provisions of the Housing Act 1988.

In addition to the above statutory developments, there is a growing realisation that the survival and future prosperity of local government require a fundamental change in the basic culture of our organisations. The new culture is gaining momentum and includes:

▽   a renewed awareness that our clients come first or, as the Americans put it, 'the customer is king';
▽   the realisation that the service manager must manage all resources;
▽   in parallel with this, a demand for areas of responsibility to be more sharply defined and an increasing emphasis on individual accountability;
▽   the decentralisation of decision making and the management information necessary for it to be effective.

These initiatives are here to stay. They pose problems but equally they offer creative challenges. They will affect relationships both within an authority and between its elected members and officers, although this book is fundamentally about relationships at the officer level. A positive and creative response to the problems and challenges will see a second centenary of local government being celebrated one hundred years from now. A defensive and negative approach will add fuel to the fire which some of our detractors are only too eager to light.

David Rawlinson
Brian Tanner

Acknowledgment

Because of other pressures the production of this book has been even more spontaneous than we had originally intended. We are indebted to John Anderson and Mike Thresher, who read parts of the draft at very short notice and were able to correct at least some of our errors and omissions. We are also grateful to the Chartered Institute of Public Finance and Accountancy for allowing us to reproduce extracts from their Local Authority Finance Glossary. Special thanks to Jean Rawlinson who, against all odds, produced the typescript.

David Rawlinson
Brian Tanner

1 Financial management in context

Key points ·

▲ *Financial management is one element of the overall management matrix.*
▲ *The task of management is to achieve the organisation's objectives as effectively, economically and efficiently as possible.*
▲ *Financial management covers a wide range of functions, not all of which are carried out wholly in the CFO's (Chief Financial Officer's) department.*
▲ *Further devolution of financial management functions to the point of service delivery is desirable.*
▲ *This process should only be constrained by valid considerations of efficiency and accountability.*

Financial management functions

Management is about getting things done! A more rigorous definition is that management is concerned with the acquisition, development and utilisation of resources to achieve certain goals.

Purists might well argue that this definition is only partial because management also encompasses the process of establishing goals and, of course, reviewing performance. We accept this criticism but feel the above definition nevertheless has merit, particularly in the local government context, where establishing goals is not purely a management prerogative.

Financial management concentrates on the resource of money. This is not to deny the importance of the other resources, namely:

▽ human resources;
▽ physical resources;
▽ information and knowledge.

Indeed, money derives its significance largely because it is usually needed to acquire the other 'productive' resources.

This description should at least make it clear that financial management is not an end in itself. It is a means to an end. It is one part of the management matrix which should be helping to achieve the organisation's goals as effectively, efficiently and economically as possible. This applies to all organisations, whether in the public or the private sector.

That's all very well but what is financial management really about — what functions does it encompass? Before referring to the checklist at Appendix A, you should attempt to compile your own list. The first item might well be the payment of salaries and wages; we mention this in case you are finding it difficult to think of any useful financial management functions!

When you come to compare your list with Appendix A, you may find that a number of the items listed in the Appendix are missing from your own list. There could be various reasons for this but two, in particular, need to be emphasised at this point, namely:

(a) lack of basic awareness of financial management functions;
(b) confusion between financial management and the functions carried out by the Chief Financial Officer's (CFO's) staff.

If (a) applies and you were indeed unaware of several of the functions listed in Appendix A, particularly those in categories 1, 2 and 3, then we refer you to chapters 6–8, where you will find a description of the procedures and issues associated with each function.

Another possibility, however, is that you have listed most or all of the functions currently performed by the CFO's department in your authority. If so, you may have omitted any financial management functions which are carried out wholly or partly in other departments or indeed other organisations. For example housing rent collection may well be the responsibility of your Director of Housing, rather than your CFO. If you work in a District or Borough Council your superannuation may be dealt with by a nearby District Council (in metropolitan areas) or by the County Council.

There is a further possibility, namely that certain functions, particularly those in category 4, do not yet play a significant part in the management scheme of your authority. You will almost certainly have come across the concept of value for money but quite possibly in the shape of ad hoc corporate initiatives rather than as a routine management function. It is probably fair to say that categories 1, 2 and 3 of Appendix A represent those financial management functions which have traditionally been the prerogative of the CFO and his or her staff and are carried out by all local authorities. It is the merit of devolving these functions as far as possible to the point of service delivery that is the principal theme of this book. In our view such a process will help to maximise the long term effectiveness of local authority service provision. It should only be limited by valid considerations of efficiency and accountability.

The functions in category 4 tend to reflect some of the newer challenges facing local authority financial management. They will become commonplace during the 1990s even if they are not so at present. It is unlikely that any of these emergent functions, with the possible exception of investment management, is or will be the sole preserve of the CFO's staff.

A word about category 5; it may appear spurious to include the provision of management information as a financial management function but effective management can only take place on the basis of adequate management information. Information must be accurate, timely, relevant and intelligible; the last criterion is becoming increasingly important as decentralisation of decision-making proceeds. The crucial role of training in supporting any devolution of financial management cannot be overemphasised. One of the greatest risks during the next ten years is that the effectiveness of new management structures and procedures will be undermined by insufficient recognition of training needs, and the resources required to satisfy them. We shall reiterate this message in later chapters.

Performance review in local government is highly topical and seems to have been so for many years. It is in the area of performance measurement that a distinction has to be made in financial management terms between the public and private sectors. In the private sector money is widely used to measure the success of an organisation. Goals and results are usually expressed in cash terms with respect to profit, output, sales, dividends or return on capital employed. These criteria are either unavailable or irrelevant in many parts of the public sector. In the past this has meant that there has been a tendency in the public sector to concentrate on resource inputs which can be converted into the common denominator of money, rather than on output or effectiveness. The Chartered Institute of Public Finance and Accountancy (CIPFA), the Audit Commission and others have striven for a number of years to develop techniques for performance measurement in local government. There are signs that these initiatives are at last beginning to bear fruit and we consider that this issue will be at or near the top of the financial management agenda during the 1990s. It is discussed further in chapters 3, 8 and 10.

Achieving effective financial management

Effective management can never be guaranteed because it involves decision making by human beings. However, there are certain conditions which will encourage effective management within an organisation and they are as important for financial management as for any other sphere of management. They are necessary whatever management structure is in place and include:

▽   the existence of clear objectives at all levels of management;
▽   well-defined levels of authority and responsibility throughout the management structure;
▽   easy access to accurate, up-to-date and understandable management information;
▽   sensible and straightforward control and reporting procedures;
▽   access to proper training and advice;
▽   the employment of effective systems for monitoring performance.

These requirements apply whether all the financial management functions listed in Appendix A are carried out by a central finance department or not. However, it is fairly easy to see that, where certain financial management functions are decentralised and particularly where responsibilities are shared between service departments and the CFO's department, these criteria will be even more crucial and yet at the same time more difficult to achieve. For example, many authorities, including our own, possess financial information systems which are satisfactory where the user is a qualified accountant or accounting technician, but are less than ideal for non-finance users. Such systems are proving more and more problematic as the decentralisation of financial management gathers pace.

Within local government the situation is further complicated by the spread of financial decision making across three levels, namely:

▽   the individual establishment;

∇   the service department; and
∇   the CFO's department.

Managers at each of these levels will have differing perspectives, needs and priorities. In terms of objectives, the establishment manager and, to a lesser extent, the service department manager may well be more concerned about effective service delivery than about the economic and efficient use of resources. Information needs will clearly differ in terms of both the level of detail and the format and content of reports. The establishment manager will want maximum freedom of action and therefore minimal financial controls, whereas the service department manager and the financial manager in the CFO's department may place greater emphasis on adequate controls over such measures as budget transfers (virement) and carry forwards. Training needs will clearly differ. These issues are considered in chapter 3.

The above differences have been brought into even sharper focus by the progressive exposure of local authority services to statutory competitive tendering. There is now a wide range of services for which local authorities are required to test their in-house operations in the market place, and to apply private sector measures of financial performance such as return on capital employed. This has necessitated a fundamental reappraisal and redefinition of objectives, responsibilities and controls and a thorough review of information and training needs. Chapter 4 will focus on these new challenges.

In the face of such major developments it is important to stress that there is no question of any of the financial management functions in Appendix A becoming obsolete or unnecessary. The role of financial management is very much intact. What is beginning to change is the approach to financial management, and especially the structural and procedural framework within which it is exercised. By the end of the 1990s we believe that financial management structures and methods will be very different from those that represent the state of the art today.

2 The chief financial officer's role

Key points

▲ *The chief financial officer (CFO) has a wide ranging statutory responsibility to ensure financial integrity (probity).*
▲ *Initiatives to devolve financial management, whether imposed by legislation or not, must avoid any material loss of probity.*
▲ *Subject to this the CFO can relinquish direct control of many financial management functions as long as effective monitoring procedures are in place.*
▲ *Certain core functions must be retained centrally under the direct control of the CFO.*
▲ *These functions relate to the co-ordination of budgeting, final accounts and certain internal audit work, the control and development of corporate IT systems, financial training and technical tasks, such as insurance.*

Introduction

Whenever financial management in local government is under discussion, the role of the Chief Financial Officer (CFO) is crucial to the debate. Sensible conclusions will only emerge if those involved recognise that there are well defined statutory powers and legal precedents, which give the CFO clear and very wide responsibilities in relation to the financial affairs of the local authority.

This is sometimes a bone of contention with both councillors and service departments and it is important that:

▽ non-finance managers understand the background to these responsibilities; and
▽ they appreciate the starting point from which any changes to existing financial procedures must be negotiated.

Inevitably CFOs are keen to guard the status and authority which these responsibilities provide and it is very clear that the general integrity and financial standing of local government in the past are largely due to the way CFOs have tackled their duties. Few people would claim that financial processes in local government were unsatisfactory in terms of integrity or probity. Whether they would be so content in terms of value for money or the provision of timely and relevant information is another matter. It is probably safe to argue that neither the elected member, nor the public generally, would want to see the financial probity of local government dissipated. The overall aim must therefore be to improve effectiveness without any material loss of probity.

Statutory responsibilities

There are three main elements to the statutory responsibilities of a CFO. These can be summarised briefly as follows:

▽ **The case of *Attorney General v De Winton* in 1906**
This case established that the CFO has a direct fiduciary relationship with rate-payers. He cannot plead that he is acting under the instruction of the Council as an excuse for an illegal act. Subsequently, the 'Wednesbury Case' developed this principle by providing for a local authority's actions to be challenged in the courts on the grounds of unreasonableness as well as illegality. Clearly this places an added onus on the CFO who effectively has to provide the ultimate authorisation for any expenditure by signing the cheque.

▽ **Section 151 of the Local Government Act 1972**
Section 151 imposes a clear statutory responsibility on the CFO. It requires that 'every local authority shall make arrangements for the proper administration of their financial affairs and shall secure that one of their officers has responsibility for the administration of those affairs'. An immediate consequence of this statute was that more prominence was given to internal audit. Financial regulations, which are the formal means of giving effect to these statutory duties within a local authority, were generally revised at this time and have since remained unchanged in many authorities until the last year or so.

▽ **Section 114 of the Local Government Finance Act 1988**
There is now a duty on every CFO to report directly to elected members if he or she believes an illegal act might take place or if expenditure might exceed available resources. This is very much a précis of the words of the Act and there has yet to be a test case in a court of law. Cases will undoubtedly emerge to clarify matters and the CFO is in a delicate and exposed position when he or she has to challenge the intentions of the Council in this way.

It is very important to understand that this statutory framework places the CFO in a position quite different from that of a finance director in a private or public company or in most other public authorities. The CFO must ensure that arrangements are in place to cover his or her statutory responsibilities. These arrangements may take the form of written manuals and procedures, regulations or minimum standards. Inevitably, they increase the cost of financial arrangements in local authorities. This is one reason why local authority overhead costs may be higher than for their private sector counterparts and also why the process of financial management may appear cumbersome and onerous to service managers and councillors.

The scope of a CFO's responsibilities

The wording of the 1972 Act is sufficiently comprehensive to embody all financial transactions that take place in a local authority. The CFO's responsibilities therefore cover a major proportion of a local authority's operations. On the other hand, there has to be some trade off between probity and efficiency; otherwise arrangements could become so riddled with costly checks that they would become inefficient to operate. It is the responsibility of the CFO to determine the extent and nature of these trade offs. Risk analysis, particularly in relation to the audit function, is therefore an increasingly common feature of financial management procedures.

A major point that non-finance managers should understand however is that, although the CFO carries the responsibility, he or she may not need to use his or her own staff to undertake the work. CFOs have widely differing views on this. One only has to observe the varying degrees to which the finance function has already been decentralised, and the variety of methods used, to realise that there is no conventional wisdom on this issue. This issue recurs frequently in the pages that follow.

The range of financial management functions which are likely to be carried out in a local authority is listed in Appendix A and described in more detail in chapters 6–8. Some of these functions, particularly those in Categories 1, 2 and 3 of Appendix A, flow directly from the CFO's statutory responsibilities. They must therefore either be under the direct control of the CFO or be carried out in accordance with his or her requirements.

Core functions

The remainder of this chapter is a description of what we feel should be the core financial functions in a regime where there is devolution of financial management. They can be defined as the financial management functions which the CFO should always carry out directly and not delegate to another department. The possibility of other agencies undertaking this work is considered in chapter 9.

In general, we believe that the CFO can fulfil his or her responsibilities by setting minimum financial standards for the provision of all financial management functions. Alongside these standards the CFO must create monitoring and reporting procedures to confirm that the organisation is functioning safely and efficiently in financial management terms or to enable corrective action to be taken. This should become the CFO's prime duty and would make it possible for the CFO to relinquish much of the routine financial work which his or her staff have traditionally performed. Within this general framework there are two types of financial management function over which the CFO is likely to retain direct control:

▽ **Co-ordination**
There is an important co-ordinating role associated with preparing the overall capital and revenue budgets and the final accounts. This task will always have to be centralised, even if the vast majority of detailed work is done outside the CFO's department. There will also be a need for a

corporate financial input into the strategic planning process, if the authority has one.

▽ **Technical**

Functions of a corporate or technical nature, such as rate and community charge collection, VAT, insurance, cash flow and borrowing, are best retained within the core. Firstly, there are unlikely to be sufficient skills in other departments to carry out such specialised work effectively and secondly there are economies of scale to be gained by central provision. A similar argument could be made for superannuation administration, where expertise is already concentrated in one tier of local authority.

The above approach envisages a large proportion of financial processing being undertaken by service departments. This immediately gives rise to a further issue, namely the division of duties between the service department and individual establishments. The principle should, in our view, be to locate financial management functions as near as possible to the point of service delivery. This is discussed in later chapters. Devolution could encompass most elements of the payroll, creditor payments, housing benefits, income, financial planning, bugetary control and final accounts functions, as well as any statutory returns and grant claims which relate to a single service.

Internal audit

There is no reference to internal audit in this scenario. We believe that some elements of internal audit work, as defined at present, could be operated quite satisfactorily within the context of a service department. This is a clear example of the trade off between probity and efficiency. Ideally, to ensure probity, all internal audit work should be entirely independent of the service manager. However, how often do we hear that internal audit should be an arm of management? Provided the auditor does not have a conflict of interest and there are reasonable checks built into the system, there seems no reason why some service activities should not be audited by a member of the same service department. The CFO should establish at the outset that all financial personnel in the service department can give objective and unfettered advice to service management and, if the occasion merits it, have direct access to the CFO. This is no different in principle from the internal auditor in the CFO's department having direct access to the Chief Executive or Chairman of the Finance Committee, when he or she wishes to question the CFO's actions. We are aware that the subject of internal audit independence is controversial and that there will be considerable debate on this issue.

This is one of several areas of financial management where experienced finance staff, who are becoming increasingly scarce, can work in harmony with non-finance staff. Many large private companies are organised in this way. It can be argued that such an organisation is likely to achieve more in the field of value for money than the traditional centralised local authority.

The extent to which internal audit can be decentralised is limited more by practicalities than by issues of principle. For example, there is a requirement for an audit programme to be drawn up. It is not appropriate for this to be done by service managers on their own although it should be done in conjunction with them. Once in place, this programme would probably have to be undertaken by two sets of people. The basic audit work could be done by finance staff or appropriately trained non-finance staff in the service department. The more complicated and higher risk work, certainly that involving computer systems and processes, would need to be done by specialist staff from the CFO's department. These staff would in fact have four functions:

▽   to approve, monitor and report on the service departments' annual audit programme;
▽   to carry out some of this work themselves, particularly in relation to computer processes and the associated controls;
▽   to set overall audit standards, train personnel and monitor the quality of audit work carried out;
▽   to liaise closely with the external auditors.

This central audit team should be experienced, qualified and highly trained but small in number. One of its major functions would be to monitor national developments in audit standards and to train staff throughout the departments accordingly.

In view of the shift in emphasis from probity to efficiency and effectiveness, this system would need to incorporate severe sanctions against any member of a service department's finance staff who was found to be shirking the difficult responsibility of giving totally objective and unfettered advice. It is important for everyone to understand these possible difficulties. They are not dissimilar to the difficulties a CFO may have to face in relation to the new Section 114 duties in the Local Government Finance Act 1988.

Budget and accounts preparation

Relationships on the side of accountancy and budget preparation are likely to be more straightforward. For these functions, the CFO would retain a small, highly qualified core team to:

▽   review and advise on the corporate financial strategy;
▽   prepare the local authority revenue budget each year and calculate, where necessary, the resources needed to finance it;
▽   prepare the local authority capital budget and advise on how this should be funded;
▽   monitor both budgets, in overall terms, during the course of the year;
▽   prepare the final accounts and see them through the external audit process;
▽   prepare those returns and statistics which can only be done centrally.

In order to be able to co-ordinate this work and consolidate meaningful figures, it is important that this team of people should set the accounting standards and guidelines for all departments to follow. There must be a very clear central direction of the consolidation process, whether the exercise is budget preparation, budget monitoring or final account preparation. However, it should not be necessary for the CFO's staff to dictate or standardise the financial information used by service managers, although there is advantage in making the crossover between the CFO's requirements and those of the service manager as simple as possible.

The other major role for the central accountancy team would, as for the central audit team, be one of training. It would be expected to keep up with best practice and hold regular training seminars with the relevant finance staff in service departments. Many organisations already use chief or development accountants to perform this function in relation to finance department staff.

Exchequer functions

The major areas of delegation and decentralisation will be in relation to the exchequer functions of payroll, creditors and income. Developments in information technology will eventually make redundant the physical movement of pieces of paper, like timesheets and invoices, between establishments or officers. Direct input by establishments will make the processes much more efficient. However, the risk factor will also increase; hence there will need to be an increased effort to ensure probity.

The CFO will need to be satisfied that:

(a) the central internal audit team has sufficient resources and expertise to ensure that the exchequer computer systems are secure;
(b) there are controls within the exchequer functions which will enable corporate objectives to be met; and
(c) new developments, either locally or nationally, are capable of effective implementation.

We have already dealt with item (a) above. As for (b), there is a need to retain the kind of role that payroll and payments section managers currently perform, such as co-ordinating the implementation of national pay awards. In addition most organisations have performance standards such as:

▽ paying 95 % of all invoices received within six weeks;
▽ income arrears should be within 5 % of the gross debit within two months of despatch of the bill;
▽ complaints should not exceed 0.1 % of the number of transactions.

This kind of information has to be collected, analysed and monitored. A central resource is therefore required.

It is envisaged that computerised systems like the payments and payroll systems will be corporate. System enhancements and changes will affect, or be capable of being used by, all departments. It will be a core function to advise on developments and on priority for implementation, after proper consultation with users.

Finally, any central exchequer resource should:

▽ set and monitor exchequer standards;
▽ lead in the training and development of exchequer personnel;
▽ co-ordinate any exchequer changes required by legislation or national developments e.g. national pay awards, changes in national insurance regulations.

There will be a close relationship between the CFO's internal audit team and these other core personnel, particularly in relation to exchequer systems. Clearly, the latter will be involved in developing the systems to provide new facilities whilst the internal audit team will be checking their security and, to a lesser extent, efficiency. Close co-operation from the outset should bring corporate benefits.

The CFO's core functions are now complete. In our view they comprise:

▽   an audit co-ordination, control and training team;
▽   a budget and accountancy co-ordination, control and training team;
▽   an exchequer co-ordination, control, training and systems development team;
▽   specialist functions which might include:
    —   Superannuation;
    —   Rate/community charge collection;
    —   VAT administration;
    —   Insurance;
    —   Cash flow management;
    —   Debt management;
    —   Investment management.

Some of us believe that this is how the CFO's department will develop over the next five years or so. Other chapters in this book will examine why this should be so and how local authority managers might approach the major changes which it implies.

3 Devolving financial management

Key points

▲ *The current emphasis on decentralisation of decision making provides the opportunity for total management at the point of service delivery.*
▲ *In order for devolved financial management to be effective:*
 ▽ *Traditional financial control and reporting procedures must be streamlined and made more flexible.*
 ▽ *Objectives and responsibilities must be clearly defined.*
 ▽ *Financial information for local managers may have to be adapted and improved.*
 ▽ *Considerable financial training and guidance will be required by local managers.*
▲ *As devolution proceeds, effective monitoring and review of financial performance will become even more important.*

Introduction

Recent legislation on competitive tendering and local management in the education service has accelerated an already evident drift in local government towards the decentralisation of decision making. The problems posed by this process of change have been aired briefly in chapter 2. In this chapter we aim to explore in more detail the opportunities and risks which are starting to face managers in local authority establishments and service departments as devolution of financial management proceeds.

Broadly speaking the opportunity is for these managers to have effective control over all the resources they employ — personnel, property, money and information — and hence the ability to exercise total management. The risk is that total management at or near the point of service delivery will be inefficient, uneconomic and ultimately ineffective. This will occur if:

▽ existing control and reporting procedures are not adjusted to meet the new requirements; and/or
▽ local managers base their decisions on inadequate awareness, expertise and information concerning the parameters and constraints within which they must operate.

The discussion in this chapter is based on a typical local authority scenario in which a service department supports a number of outside establishments.

Although the establishments will probably be the main service providers, it is quite possible that the service department will also have some responsibilities for direct service provision. The education service within a county council or metropolitan district council is a good example. Schools, colleges and other outside education establishments will be the main service providers, but some important services, such as student awards and school transport administration, are likely to be delivered from the centre. In the remainder of this chapter we shall use the term 'managers' to cover all those who have direct responsibility for service provision, whether based centrally within service departments or in outside establishments. We shall also refer to budget holders; these are, or should be, individual managers who have the responsibility both for managing a particular service activity and for controlling expenditure on that activity against the amounts provided in the annual revenue budget. Budget holders can operate either in service departments or in outside establishments but it is essential that there is one and only one budget holder for each part of the budget and that there are clear guidelines for determining responsibilities.

The direct impact of the legislation now being implemented is confined to a fairly narrow range of financial management functions. For example, local management of schools (LMS) devolves responsibility for major aspects of financial planning and budgetary control from the centre to individual governing bodies and heads. There is no statutory requirement at present for local education authorities to devolve any other financial management functions to LMS schools, although information regarding the costs of financial and other support services will have to be provided to schools.

The purpose of these comments is not to play down the significance of LMS; the authors are both sufficiently involved in its implementation in Somerset to appreciate the scale of the task. Indeed most of the subsequent discussion will concentrate on the issues raised by development of precisely this sort. However, it is important to remember that many important financial mangement functions, such as payroll, creditor payments and internal audit, may not immediately be affected by the recent statutory initiatives. What the legislation on competitive tendering and local management is certainly bringing to the fore is interest in the effectiveness and efficiency with which all financial management functions are carried out, and of course their cost.

Current problems

At present, management decisions in local authorities are subject to various constraints. Some of these constraints are formal, explicit and relate primarily to financial management issues. These include:

▽ **Policy**
    Managers are subject to the policy decisions of elected members and to financial plans, usually in the form of capital and annual revenue budgets, which are approved in order to implement those decisions. In addition there are various procedural constraints whose main purpose is to limit the ability of managers to depart from the approved policies. A good example is the treatment of virement. In most local authorities there are strict rules which must be followed if a manager wishes to use money voted for one

part of the budget, e.g. equipment, to spend in another part of the budget, e.g. staff.

▽ **Probity**

Alongside and often interlinking with the policy constraints are the formal rules which are usually set out in financial regulations and which enable the CFO to fulfil the statutory responsiblities described in the previous chapter. These regulations may cover such diverse activities as handling petty cash and authorising a major capital project.

There is no doubt that the administrative structures and processes which have been established to cope with these characteristics of local government, namely the role of elected members and the need for probity, have rendered local authority decision making more bureaucratic and often time consuming, especially by comparison with some parts of the private sector. Even before the advent of recent legislation, many were beginning to question whether the entire paraphernalia of controls embodied in standing orders and financial regulations were necessary as they stood to safeguard the authority of members and the peace of mind of the CFO. More significantly perhaps there was an increasing recognition that certain controls should be loosened in order to achieve a better balance between probity and effectiveness.

The opportunities

In financial management terms what recent legislation has sought to do is to oblige local authorities to concentrate on:

▽   establishing service objectives in output terms for the areas affected;
▽   providing sufficient overall cash resources to enable these objectives to be achieved economically and efficiently; and
▽   monitoring the extent to which the objectives are in fact achieved.

This is far removed from the detailed objectives and tight controls, invariably expressed in terms of resource inputs, which are embodied in the traditional annual revenue budget and the financial regulations that govern budget holders. At present most budget holders are not merely constrained to a spending total, but instead face separate and specific limits on what they can spend in each area of their budget — professional staff, support staff, premises costs, transport costs, supplies and services and so on. Indeed in certain key areas such as staffing there may well be total control by the centre so that the budget holder has little or no discretion regarding recruitment, levels of pay or service conditions.

In direct service organisations, schools with delegated budgets and further education colleges these detailed controls can no longer be applied. As well as having a clear knowledge of the total resources available to them, managers will have considerable flexibility as to how those resources are applied. Virements and carry forwards from one financial year to the next will be possible without reference to the centre. Establishments will no longer be obliged to obtain goods and services from suppliers nominated by County Hall. At the formal level, therefore, total management at the point of service delivery will become a practical possibility rather than a distant ideal.

At first sight, there are few clouds on the horizon for the managers concerned. It is certainly true that automatic central funding in full of pay awards and general inflation will not necessarily apply to devolved budgets, even if it did before, and this could cause some local discomfort. However, the major loser here seems to be the CFO whose statutory responsibilities with regard to these activities remain but who has lost many of the detailed controls currently deemed necessary to fulfil them. In our view the best strategy for the CFO under these circumstances is to define and monitor sensible minimum standards and also to ensure that managers are provided with appropriate training, guidance and information so that their financial management is both imaginative and sound.

The risks

In most local authorities the formal constraints under which managers currently operate are compounded by variety of informal blocks and brakes. These include:

▽   The absence of clear objectives;
▽   Blurred responsibilities and accountabilities;
▽   A shortage of useful and timely management information;
▽   Even more restrictive and cumbersome control and reporting procedures than are legitimately required for reasons of policy and probity;
▽   Inadequate access to training and advice;
▽   A total absence of performance review.

Each of these is a serious barrier to effective management. Together they represent an environment in which attempts to decentralise decision-making must surely founder even if they have statutory backing.

The need for clear objectives is now so well recognised that little further comment ought to be needed. However, formalising and communicating objectives is a difficult and time consuming exercise in a large organisation because there needs to be a hierarchy of compatible and consistent objectives to overlay the organisation's management structure. Each manager should understand clearly what he or she is expected to achieve and how this will contribute to achieving the overall objectives of the organisation. Initial forays into this area can easily become bogged down and then take second place to more urgent management commitments. Our advice would be to persevere to the end but not to aim for perfection first time round; there will be ample opportunity for refinement when objectives are reviewed, as they must be periodically.

So far in this chapter our discussion has covered all managers with direct responsibility for service provision. However, there are many managers within service departments, and even a few within larger establishments, who are not directly involved in service provision but who exercise some sort of co-ordinating, advisory or supervisory role. Under these circumstances it is very easy for financial management responsibilities to become blurred. If this occurs effective financial management will be much more difficult to achieve, particularly for certain key control functions such as budgeting and budgetary control.

Given the high incidence of centralised mainframe financial systems in local government, it is likely that most centrally located local authority managers will have access to a plentiful supply of financial information. Whether this information is relevant, up-to-date or easy to understand is another matter. Managers in outside establishments may be even less fortunate. This topic will be covered more fully in chapter 5.

In all organisations systems and procedures are governed not only by current requirements but also by precedent and tradition. The temptation to stick with familiar methods can never be underestimated. Even where there is willingness to move with the times, the increasing pace of change in local government can make it difficult in practice to do so. If financial control procedures are to remain credible, they must be continually reviewed and adapted in the light of statutory changes, new demands on services and improvements in information technology. Otherwise they will eventually become discredited in the eyes of non-finance managers, and will then be evaded or totally ignored.

If certain financial management functions and decisions are to be devolved successfully to staff who are not financially qualified and have little or no previous experience of financial management, some training is obviously necessary. The introduction of local management in schools provides a very clear illustration of the considerable training burden which is created by the need to spread financial awareness and expertise across a numerically large, varied and widely dispersed group. Although such a commitment is almost certainly beyond the immediate resources of the CFO and his or her staff, the fact remains that a much greater proportion of the CFO's resources will need to be devoted to training during the 1990s than has been the case in the past.

The point has already been made that, in financial terms, reviewing performance is much more straightforward in the private sector than in the public sector. Nevertheless the nettle of performance review has to be grasped; otherwise the entire process may lose direction and purpose. As with objective setting we would recommend a pragmatic approach which builds over time on the possibly small number of performance indicators which are both relevant and, at least at the outset, capable of being measured. Information technology has an important part to play in the development of performance indicators. The increasing capability of IT systems to capture, store, analyse and present both financial and non-financial data is almost certainly the key to ultimate success. However, there is still a long way to go for most of us!

Some solutions

As stated earlier the existence of any one of the problems highlighted above will seriously hamper efforts to devolve financial management. A combination of them could well prove fatal, despite the strictures of government legislation and the best intentions of both finance and non-finance managers. Any strategy for decentralisation must therefore ensure that the relevant issues have been addressed. Based on our own experience, in theory if not yet in practice, we would commend the following package of measures as a significant first step in this direction:

▽ introduce or resurrect a corporate strategy document which includes agreed service objectives;

▽   encourage all departments to prepare their own business plans;
▽   review the management structures throughout the organisation and adapt
     them to fit the requirements of the 1990s;
▽   rewrite standing orders and financial regulations to reflect the realities of
     the new era (see chapter 4);
▽   review the management information systems (and particularly the
     financial information systems) within the organisation and develop a
     flexible corporate strategy for their development (see chapter 5);
▽   institute a formal staff review and development scheme throughout the
     organisation;
▽   link this with a coordinated and properly resourced training programme
     for staff, with particular emphasis on management training;
▽   introduce service level agreements to cover all support services;
▽   employ small multi-disciplinary working groups to tackle major corporate
     issues.

This seems a formidable list but many local authorities will already have
adopted some of these measures and there may be some authorities that have
done all this and much more. It is interesting to note that corporate initiatives
feature in the above list. What is increasingly clear to us is that success in
decentralising decision making in local authorities will require both a major
corporate effort and the retention of an influential, if not numerically strong,
central core.

4 Competitive services

Key points

▲ *The extension of compulsory competitive tendering (CCT) poses a major challenge to finance personnel and systems.*

▲ *CCT imposes a new business culture on those directly involved, including managers providing support services to direct service organisations (DSOs).*

▲ *The need to split the client and contractor responsibilities necessitates new structures and relationships in service areas subject to CCT.*

▲ *If a DSO is to be dissuaded from carrying out financial management functions in-house, or acquiring them from an external agency, the CFO must provide:*
  ▽ *efficient exchequer services;*
  ▽ *expert advice on business planning and forecasting;*
  ▽ *relevant and timely costing information; and*
  ▽ *adequate technical support;*
  at a competitive price.

▲ *CFOs should aim to produce a single set of financial regulations which are appropriate for all areas of the local authority, including DSOs.*

Introduction

It is sometimes difficult to appreciate that compulsory competitive tendering (CCT) has been part of the local authority scene since 1980. The Local Government Planning and Land Act 1980 brought competition into the areas of housing repairs, highway maintenance and sewerage agency work. Direct labour organisations (DLOs) were established in most local authorities to compete for work which had previously been theirs by right. The vast majority of those DLOs are still in business today. Under the 1988 Local Government Act, CCT has been extended to:

▽ schools and welfare catering;
▽ refuse collection;
▽ vehicle maintenance;
▽ grounds maintenance;
▽ street cleaning;
▽ cleaning of buildings;
▽ management of sports and leisure facilities.

Although this major extension of CCT is being introduced in phases, we are now very much in the age of the Direct Service Organisation (DSO).

The purpose of this historical background is to demonstrate

▽ that competition within local authority services is not new — indeed many of our services outside the field of law, order and public protection have faced some private sector competition for a considerable time, e.g. car parking, leisure facilities;

▽   that CCT now affects a large and increasing number of local authority employees.

The other point to be made by way of introduction is that CCT is no longer a transparently cosmetic exercise. It profoundly affects the way in which services have to be managed, both in financial and non-financial terms. It may be some time before many of us experience CCT, either willingly or under duress, but no manager in local government can be sure of escape in the long term. The need for some appreciation of what CCT is all about is therefore vital.

In this chapter we shall examine the considerable additional demands which CCT places on the management resources of a local authority, and how these demands are being met, particularly on the finance side. The picture that emerges may not be a complete blueprint for the 1990s but we believe that many aspects of CCT will permeate other areas of local government in the coming years, irrespective of legislative developments.

The new culture

It is all too easy to become immediately engrossed in the structural, procedural and technical changes associated with CCT. In many ways the most important change brought about by CCT has been in attitude or culture. DLO and DSO managers face the reality that failure to:

▽   compete with the private sector, or
▽   win the tender, or
▽   make a profit, or
▽   meet the Secretary of State's required rate of return,

could ultimately lead to the organisation going out of business and to redundancy for their staff and themselves. It should be no surprise therefore that they are extremely cost conscious, or that they expect prompt information and advice. Finance managers involved directly in providing support to DLOs and DSOs are now fully aware of this challenge, not least because their livelihood is at stake as well. However, it is important that those on the periphery of CCT recognise this new business culture and are prepared for the demands and tensions that it can produce.

New structures

The basic overriding principle is that a local authority must organise itself so that genuine competition not only exists, but is seen to exist. Failure to pay attention to this obvious, but not always accepted point, can not only incur the ill-will of interested parties, but might needlessly involve the Secretary of State in the process.

The main agencies involved in the financial management of CCT are:

▽   the client;

▽ the client agent;
▽ the DSO (or DLO);
▽ the Chief Financial Officer (CFO) of the local authority;
▽ the external auditor;
▽ the Secretary of State;
▽ the DSO Board (or its equivalent).

Each will be considered in turn.

The client

The client is the local authority which is responsible for providing a particular service. Usually detailed regulations are laid down e.g. basic nutritional and hygiene standards for school meals or the number and standard of grass cuts for grounds maintenance. The local authority normally devolves these responsibilities to standing committees and at this point each local authority can be different in its organisation. The important point is that the client is responsible for:

▽ determining the qualitative and quantitive standards of provision that will be set out in the tender documentation;
▽ monitoring those standards during the course of the contract (quality control);
▽ paying the contractor for services provided.

The client agent

There may not always be a need for a separate client agent. However, if the local authority does not carry out the client function corporately, it may appoint an agent department which has the relevant expertise, or which can pull together various aspects of the same type of provision for the local authority as a whole. Good examples would be the Engineers Department for vehicle maintenance and Property Services Department for grounds maintenance. The exact terms of reference will be determined by the client, but usually most elements will be delegated and the client will hold the agent responsible for enforcing the appropriate standards, and meeting all tender requirements and contractual payments, which will subsequently be recharged to the client.

The DSO

The DSO will provide the actual service or operation within the specified terms of the tender. It will be monitored for quantity and quality by the client, or its agent, and will have to deliver the service at the price agreed. Variations to the contract are clearly negotiable and there are likely to be clauses as to how inflation will be treated. The DSO will make a profit or loss at the end of the period, which may not be in accordance with its budget. It will provide its financial and advisory services itself, unless it has an agreement with the local authority to buy services from it. We will return to this point later.

The chief financial officer (CFO)

The CFO has a statutory role, already discussed in chapter 2, in relation to the financial administration of the local authority. He or she has to be satisfied that safe and efficient arrangements are made for financial affairs and this must include the DSO's affairs, as it is still legally part of the local authority There has to be a financial management objective which takes account of what might be two conflicting aspects:

▽ from DSO's viewpoint — providing effective financial support at minimum cost; and
▽ from CFO's viewpoint — achieving an effective financial management framework which pays due regard to probity, internal check, public accountability and those other matters already discussed.

Both parties should have efficiency and value for money as combined objectives. Subsequent sections of this chapter will discuss how this potential conflict can be minimised.

The external auditor

The auditor is likely to be the local authority auditor which should minimise audit fees. The auditor's certificate and report for the DSO should be separate from those for the the rest of the local authority. The auditor has to report certain matters to the Secretary of State.

The Secretary of State

The Secretary of State has considerable powers within the enabling legislation and through regulations which can be issued. Probably the most important is the power to set profit targets for DSOs in relation to the return on capital employed (ROCE) and to require a DSO to be wound up if it consistently fails to meet the target. This is not the place to discuss these powers in detail but it is essential to understand the vital importance of ensuring prudent and efficient financial management to enable these targets to be met.

The DSO Board

Many, but not all, authorities have established boards to oversee the activities of their DSOs. We shall not attempt to describe the different formats, but will simply outline the likely composition of such a body and the major responsibilities that it might assume.
It is likely to be:

▽ small in number;
▽ representative of all parties;
▽ comprised of councillors, and advised by a minimum number of officers, typically Chief Executive, CFO, and Personnel Officer.

Its responsibilities could include:

▽ approving a business plan;

▽   deciding whether a DSO will submit a tender;
▽   deliberating over personnel policies;
▽   advising the local authority on distribution/retention of future profits;

New relationships

New attitudes and structures inevitably forge new and interesting
relationships and CCT has generated more than its fair share of these. The
most severe and long-standing problem which local authorities have had to face
since CCT was first introduced is the difficulty of separating the client role
from the contractor (DSO) role in organisations where the two have
traditionally been performed by the same managers.

Having to establish two separate management organisations to achieve
what was previously accomplished by one seems an odd way of increasing
efficiency. Many local authorities started from this viewpoint in the early 1980s
and have attempted to operate with at least some of their managers wearing
both a client and a DSO hat. The problems with this approach have been
considerable if not unexpected. The tender preparation, tender submission
and evaluation processes are especially difficult for anyone with dual
responsibilities. Quality control and performance monitoring are also fraught
with difficulty.

This problem also affects support functions, including and especially
finance in particular. 'Chinese walls' abound in the CFO's department as
services to the DSO and the client are redefined and, as far as possible,
separated. Data access and security are a particularly contentious issue. Many
DSO managers are extremely unhappy if they find that members of CFO's
staff who provide financial advice to the client have easy access to financial
information concerning the DSO.

The new relationships within local authorities inspired by CCT are still
evolving. Unfortunately, one relationship that has not changed sufficiently is
that between a local authority DSO and the outside world. Because the DSO is
part of its parent local authority, it is prevented from competing in the private
sector market, unless it does so purely to utilise spare capacity. The absence of
unfettered two way competition is a considerable, and in our view, unjust
burden on DSOs.

New procedures and techniques

In order to operate effectively, the DSO manager will need to be in control of
all elements of the DSO budget. Subject to tender requirements and legal
restrictions, there should be complete freedom of choice in determining the
resources that are employed to achieve the DSO's objectives. This freedom
should encompass:

▽   personnel policies including:
     — redundancy,
     — performance or productivity bonuses,
     — short term lay offs,

— benefits in kind, as long as these are relatively typical of the industry within which the DSO is competing;

▽ the abandonment of establishment controls — in relation to a ceiling placed on maximum numbers employed;

▽ local determination of building and equipment maintenance activities, unless the client has provided the building and has specified to all contractors a form of maintenance liability which has to be followed.

This flexibility should extend to the DSO manager's right to use whatever professional adviser he or she requires in these specialist areas. If the local authority specialist is used, this should in our view be on the basis of a proper service level agreement which sets out quality and quantity of service to be provided (see chapter 9 for a detailed discussion of SLAs).

Financial procedures

Until a management buyout takes it into the private sector, a DSO is still part of its parent authority. The retention of local authority status imposes a number of financial restrictions on DSOs. These include:

▽ the need for CFO approval to incur capital expenditure (unless met from revenue or reserve funds after April 1990);

▽ the parallel need for CFO approval to borrow (except possibly on a day to day basis);

▽ the continued right of all employees to belong to the local authority superannuation fund;

▽ the CFO's control over internal audit arrangements.

Most other financial arrangements within which DSOs operate will be matters for negotiation. In some areas agreement between the DSO manager and the CFO may not be easy to achieve. If differing views about the most appropriate arrangements cannot be reconciled, the external auditor may have a significant, though initially informal, role to play. The auditor's advice should be heeded because he or she will be in a difficult position to give a 'presents fairly' certificate to the accounts if there is any doubt about whether adequate financial arrangements have been made.

There are a number of areas of financial support to DSOs which are particularly complex and potentially contentious. These include:

▽ financial systems and the role of information technology generally;

▽ financial planning, accountancy and technical support, e.g. insurance, cash flow;

▽ financial regulations.

Financial systems and information technology

Local authorities are very large concerns. Almost all, if not all, have computerised financial systems with varying degrees of centralisation. There is a growing awareness that establishments and DSOs want more current and relevant information and facilities for the local manipulation of data. This requirement will take time to deliver. In addition, there will always be a need to integrate and consolidate the establishment or DSO information at the centre

B

because of the statutory requirement for the local authority as a whole to prepare:

▽   a budget;
▽   final accounts.

Therefore, whatever the arrangements for an individual DSO, it will be necessary to provide common or at least consistent information to both the centre and the DSO. This issue is exactly the same in principle as that being tackled in local management of schools (LMS) and is considered further in the next chapter.

There is pressure from DSO managers for facilities to be provided which will allow them to carry out their financial management functions locally, as if they were an independent business. This could include:

▽   the posting of entries to income and expenditure accounts;
▽   the provision of costing information;
▽   the payment of creditors;
▽   the preparation of income invoices;
▽   payroll facilities;

If such facilities cannot be provided by the corporate systems, the CFO will have three concerns:

▽   small units (e.g. DSOs) abandoning a centralised financial system will place an increased burden, in terms of unit costs, on the remaining clients;
▽   an alternative financial system is unlikely to provide financial information in the format required to consolidate the accounts without additional effort and expenditure;
▽   each financial system (and there could be several in existence) will display its own problems and inadequacies in relation to levels of internal check and effectiveness of control mechanisms.

It is therefore vital that adequate communications and interface facilities are established between central systems and remote sites, if they do not already exist. The 1990s will require much more flexible systems with a technology which can satisfy the needs of the DSO manager, and indeed other chief officers, from a corporate database. Typically, information will be current, is likely to be updated daily and will feed into flexible spreadsheet facilities which will help make it highly relevant and easy to interpret.

Charging may also need to become more flexible. This may well be necessary to deal with a situation in which a DSO manager can obtain an IT system which will satisfy his or her own needs at a lower cost than the centrally imposed corporate product. It may then be appropriate to levy a reduced corporate IT charge on the DSO, the difference being a corporate cost. Indeed, this comparison would need to take account not merely of the hardware and software costs involved, but also of the cost of communications facilities, including networking.

Financial planning, accountancy and technical support

Business planning is a relatively new enterprise for the CFO and his or her staff. It represents a radical departure from the traditional local authority budgetary processes. However it is a crucial aspect in the financial management of DSOs and must therefore be under the direct supervision of the DSO manager. In some authorities, including our own, a specialised team has been set up within the CFO's department to provide exclusive services to DSO management in this area and also in relation to budget preparation and final accounts. The need to prepare business plans with:

▽   the longer term perspective required by CCT;
▽   the emphasis on outputs rather than exclusively on inputs;
▽   inbuilt performance measures;
▽   overall resource requirements, including capital assets;
▽   a degree of flexibility

is a clear example of how the discipline of CCT has stimulated a more businesslike approach across local authorities in general. Departments not yet subject to CCT already have or are in the process of drawing up business plans to enhance their effectiveness, efficiency and long-term survival prospects. Some corporate initiatives are also under way.

An important aspect of financial planning is capital spending for the purposes of enhancing and replacing capital assets. The existing approaches to local authority asset management and capital accounting are totally inappropriate for CCT. Local authority techniques such as historic cost and debt charges are having to be replaced with private sector concepts such as replacement cost and depreciation. The situation is further complicated in certain tendering situations because the client may opt to retain ownership of the assets employed by the DSO e.g. school kitchens and catering equipment.

On the accountancy side mention must be made of costing information because this is another area where CCT imposes far greater demands than existed previously. The availability of comprehensive and up-to-date unit cost information is vital to DSO management. Existing financial systems have to be enhanced and interface facilities have to be provided with non-financial data bases to enable this information to be produced.

There are a wide variety of technical matters where the DSO manager will rely on the CFO for advice. These include:

▽   Cash flows
▽   Insurance
▽   Value added tax
▽   National insurance, sickness and other employee regulations
▽   Superannuation

Cash flow management should be dealt with by the CFO as he can obtain improved terms by aggregating all cash flows of the local authority and then negotiating from a stronger base. However, DSO managers must be fully aware of their cash flow position and the individual DSOs should receive (or pay) interest relative to their credit (or debit) position. Associated with this is the need for DSOs to have adequate working capital — another issue which rarely concerns those local authority managers not involved in CCT.

Insurance is a particularly complex issue in relation to CCT. The authority as a whole has a right and a duty to undertake certain activities:

▽   negotiate the best terms available with the insurance market by
     aggregating all demands and dealing from strength;
▽   determine the liabilities and risks that require external insurance, as all
     others will be met from internal sources (i.e. in future, the community
     charge payer). This will include uninsured losses from the DSO, if it is
     incapable of meeting those losses itself;
▽   select the appropriate insurer(s).

The local authority has a right to expect the DSO to obtain the same risk
insurance as it has itself — due to its ultimate liability. Therefore, the most
obvious course to take is to apportion its insurance premium(s) between itself
and the DSO. If the DSO can obtain a lower quotation for similar risks from an
external source, then it should pay that premium to the authority but still use
the local authority's policy cover. The reasoning here is that most local
authority policies are long-term and often have discounts built in on the basis
that all insurance should be placed with a single company. Where self-
insurance is effected, the DSO should again be entitled to pay the lowest
premium that could be found in the open market.

There is a tendency for DSO managers and others to regard the local
authority status of DSOs as a liability or a handicap. Cash flow and insurance·
are two examples where the local authority link can be advantageous, because
of the benefits of large scale in these areas of financial managements.

Financial regulations

Most of the above matters will be embodied in the local authority's financial
regulations. It is convenient to consider financial regulations in the context of
DSOs, although the issue has much wider implications. The fact is that recent
statutory developments and organisation trends are all pushing in the same
direction, namely towards more flexibility and less detailed prescription in
local authority standing orders and financial regulations. Some CFOs may
instinctively resist this pressure and, indeed may prefer comprehensive formal
controls as budgets are devolved more and more widely. As usual it is a
question of balance. The statutory responsibilities of the CFO must be
safeguarded, but not, in the case of DSOs, at the expense of commercial
viability and hence jobs.

There is no particular reason why the regulations covering the local
authority, DSOs, LMS schools, FE colleges and other establishments should
not all be the same — in principle, at least. Only absolute amounts should be
different, e.g. amounts allowed for virement, bad debt write-offs, etc.

Existing financial regulations are likely to cover:

▽   accounting and budgeting arrangements;
▽   capital expenditure and its financing;
▽   expenditure outside approved budgets;
▽   virement (switching budget provision between approved budget heads);
▽   insurance;
▽   income collection and bad debts;
▽   internal audit arrangements;
▽   banking and lending/borrowing arrangements;
▽   stores and stock accounting;

▽   provision for carry forwards of expenditure;
▽   roles and responsibilities of CFO, service chief officers, DSO managers
    and establishment heads.

Not all these headings are relevant to DSOs, e.g. virement. However, we
believe there is merit in consolidating financial regulations into a single
document as soon as possible. Regulations which are appropriate for DSOs
will probably form a suitable framework for all local authority activities in the
1990s. In our view the other objectives for the 1990s should be:

▽   to have a minimum number of regulations with minimal complexity and
    bureaucracy;
▽   to determine individuals' responsibilities at the outset, and draw up the
    regulations on that basis;
▽   to maximise the delegation of financial responsibility to the operational
    level (e.g. the DSO managers);
▽   to create the opportunity for non-finance officers to report directly to the
    CFO on certain matters.

The current wide-ranging review of financial regulations in the light of
CCT and other initiatives will provide the basis on which financial
management in the 1990s will develop and from which its ultimate
effectiveness will derive. The above objectives reflect our basic philosophy. If
the will to delegate is there, then the means will be found. Maybe the most
controversial of the objectives is the last one. Is it possible for a CFO to have
people reporting to him who are not accountants and not on his staff? We have
no doubt whatsoever that the answer is 'yes'. Appropriately enough, this
provides an opportunity for the DSO manager to achieve what must be very
dear to his or her heart, namely to reduce overhead costs for financial support.

5 Information technology

Key points

▲ Information technology has the potential to fulfil the management information needs of the 1990s.
▲ Developments in IT, including those needed to provide decentralised financial information, must be properly planned and adequately resourced.
▲ Traditional corporate financial information systems (FIS) may be inadequate to meet the needs of devolved financial management, particularly in relation to ease of access and use, flexibility, timeliness and presentation.
▲ However, devolution of financial management does not necessarily mean the total abandonment of the corporate FIS in favour of local PC based systems.
▲ If a local approach, without any direct link to corporate systems, is chosen the resource implications in terms of training, guidance, monitoring and internal audit must be recognised and provided for.

Introduction

This book contains a chapter on information technology (IT) not because local government computer installations have traditionally been part of the CFO's department, but because IT holds the key to the management information needs of the 1990s. As with many other issues covered in this book, this message applies to all areas of local authority management, not just to financial management.

After some general comments about IT development we shall concentrate on financial information systems (FIS) in local authorities. We shall not attempt to cover specialised financial applications such as community charge collection. These will be crucial to the survival and well being of all local authorities in the 1990s, but are not, in our view, relevant to the issue of devolved financial management which is the central theme of this book.

There will be no attempt here to encourage the reader in any particular direction as far as IT is concerned. We do not have the technical expertise to assess the relative merits of mainframes, minis, micros and other hardware options, or techniques and systems such as networks, databases and spreadsheets. Indeed it may well be that by the late 1990s local authority IT facilities will be even more diverse than they are today. Other important issues into which we will not delve in any detail are:

▽ the cost of information technology and how this should be passed on to users; the advent of networking adds to the existing problems in this area;
▽ the corporate exchequer (feeder) systems, e.g. payroll, creditors. Their ability to cope with remote interrogation and updating is crucial if they are to support decentralised processing. Their interface with the corporate FIS may also need to be improved to meet the information needs of devolved financial management.

What we can do is bring out some of the issues which face managers who are involved in developing information systems to cope with devolved financial management. Our hope is that this will raise awareness among non-finance managers and also stress to all concerned the importance of a partnership approach to future developments. This is essential if we are to provide information systems which will enable all managers to operate effectively, efficiently and economically in the 1990s.

Managing IT developments

Developments in IT must be based on:

▽ careful planning;
▽ user involvement;
▽ a flexible approach.

In large organisations planning must be carried out within the context of a corporate IT strategy. This does not mean that developments need necessarily be restricted in the choice of hardware, software or physical configuration. It does, however, mean that they should be properly justified and prioritised on the basis of criteria agreed corporately, and co-ordinated with other developments within the organisation. Local authorities are littered with the debris of ad hoc IT developments which were not managed in this way.

At the planning stage it is important to take account of the following factors:

▽ Cost — many local authorities are severely constrained in undertaking major developments of any sort because of problems with funding. These are the result either of government controls or of concern about the burden on local tax payers, or both (see Appendices B and C). Leasing has been widely employed to overcome the existing capital controls system although this avenue has been progressively blocked in recent years. Operating leases will continue to be off-limit under the new capital control system which will apply from April 1990. Direct revenue funding will also be free from control, but the impact on community charge payers of increases in revenue spending will be even more pronounced than the impact on rate payers is at the moment.
▽ Staff resources — the availability, or rather the non-availability, of specialist IT staff is a further brake on the pace of IT developments in local government. Authorities have the options of paying the market rates for the necessary staff or of employing external consultants to assist with the design and implementation of new systems or, in the case of software, of

purchasing an applications package from an outside software house. All these options, of course, have cost implications. It should be noted that IT staff, along with architects and valuers, are the most transferrable of all local authority staff to and from the private sector.

▽ External solutions — irrespective of problems with in-house staff, the purchase of a package from a software house or another organisation may be the most cost-effective solution. It seems that the days are over when we could insist on individual tailoring of specifications for each local authority. This is increasingly the case with standard mainframe applications.

▽ Existing IT facilities — the range of available options may be limited by the existing computer configuration within a local authority. Although it is always technically possible to overcome problems of non-compatibility, the cost of doing so may be prohibitively expensive.

The necessity of involving the end-user in any IT development is so well accepted that it hardly needs to be mentioned. However, actions do not always match words and it is probably fair to say that developments involving financial information systems have a relatively poor track record. This may stem in part from the close proximity of IT staff and finance staff, with the CFO still having responsibility for both groups in many authorities. Managers outside the CFO's department may have been unable or unwilling to participate fully in FIS developments because of this, and undue priority may therefore have been given in the design of financial information systems to the CFO's need for standardisation, consolidation and control at the expense of the non-finance manager's need for clarity, flexibility and accessibility. The rapid spread of devolved financial management in local authorities is highlighting this as a serious deficiency of many corporate financial information systems.

Given a willingness to involve the end-users and, in particular, to establish their requirements at the outset, IT development managers sometimes find initially that users are not sure what they do want. The possibility that user requirements will evolve as an IT development proceeds is one of several reasons why a flexible approach is essential. Another is the likelihood, particularly with developments which have a long lead time, that hardware and/or software improvements will provide opportunities which were not available when the initial evaluation was carried out. A flexible approach will also be necessary to cope with the inevitable delays and malfunctions which are part of any IT development.

The requirements of devolved financial management

So far we have dealt with general issues which could be applied to any IT project. In the remainder of this chapter we will focus on the demands created by the devolution of financial management and how existing financial information systems might be developed to meet them.

What would a manager facing the challenge of devolved financial management expect from a FIS? We suggest that some or all of the following requirements would predominate.

▽ efficient and economical methods of data capture and storage;

▽   rapid access to all relevant data, including information in other databases
     such as property and personnel;
▽   the ability to manipulate and analyse data to produce useful management
     information;
▽   a large measure of control over the format and content of reports and
     access to facilities such as graphics to enhance presentation;
▽   the facility to combine text with financial and non-financial information in
     producing reports;
▽   automatic generation of key management information and reports;
▽   a robust, reliable and straightforward system.

Managers in local government are increasingly aware that all the above criteria can already be met by systems in use elsewhere. They also hear or read about user-friendly menu-driven micro-computer systems which, with limited training, bring these capabilities within easy reach of those who are not IT experts. More recently they may have been learning from colleagues about micro-based software packages which have been developed specifically to assist those affected by major new initiatives such as local management of schools.

Not surprisingly they are beginning to question why some of the above facilities are not yet available to them. Moreover they are less willing than before to accept that the improvements which they feel they need cannot be introduced quickly and painlessly. When faced with this sort of situation, those involved in IT systems development should avoid being panicked into hasty and ill-conceived decisions. Equally they must ensure that, as well as involving users fully in establishing system requirements, they keep users fully informed of progress with design and implementation. If nothing is happening and users are being kept in the dark, they are very likely to seek local solutions without recourse to the IT department. How often do we see this happen?

One fundamental issue is likely to recur in reviewing financial information needs as part of any initiative to devolve financial management. This has already been referred to and concerns the importance of achieving the correct balance between the user needs outlined above and the CFO's corporate need for standardisation, consolidation and control. Although it is dangerous to generalise it is probably fair to suggest that in most authorities the balance is currently in favour of the CFO's needs. It certainly has been in the past. What is equally certain is that devolving financial management will change that relationship with a far greater emphasis on user needs.

Traditional financial information systems

At present the norm in local government is still for the majority of financial transactions to be processed centrally. This is most evident in the case of the traditional exchequer functions, particularly payroll. The main advantages of the centralised approach are efficiency and probity. In the case of payroll it makes sense in efficiency terms for the expertise required to cope with the myriad of national pay agreements which cover local authority employees, and the complexities of PAYE, national insurance, statutory sick pay and maternity pay to be pooled centrally. This approach has also been in tune with the fact that most staffing establishments have until recently been directly controlled from the centre. Reliance on a corporate payroll system using a central mainframe computer has given the CFO's staff firm control over the transactions data covering three quarters of the authority's revenue spending. Not only is this the best solution in terms of ensuring that all staff are paid correctly and on time; it is also the strongest assurance of the accuracy and integrity of the payroll data which are fed into the FIS. Similar considerations apply to creditor payments and the collection of income, although for these functions the advantages of pooled expertise are not quite so compelling.

Thus the typical local authority model has been and still is of central IT systems for processing payroll, creditor payments, income and other financial transactions fed into a corporate FIS. The purposes of this system are to provide a record of all financial transactions involving the authority in the current and one or more previous years, and to consolidate these transactions in various ways in order to identify both the amounts spent in each establishment or division of service (objective classification) and the amounts spent on each subjective category (employees, premises, transport, running costs, etc.). Budget information is also fed into the system to enable comparisons to be made at various levels between expenditure or income to date and the approved budget for the year. Reports or tabulations are produced weekly or monthly or on request and are distributed to establishments and service departments in order for them to exercise budgetary control. Staff in the CFO's department, and possibly in service departments and larger establishments, will have direct access to FIS via terminals or micro-computers. They will be able to call up a range of standard enquiry screens to assist further with budget monitoring. Special routines are built into the FIS to help close the accounts at the end of each financial year, and there are also facilities within the FIS to assist in preparing the estimates for the forward financial year.

The basis of all such systems is the transaction code. We shall devote some space to explaining the structure and purpose of FIS codes because this is necessary in order to understand the capabilities and limitations of the system.

The FIS code contains the information on which the system relies to account for each transaction. Every transaction which is fed into the FIS must therefore have been allocated such a code which typically is ten or so digits long. The coding structure might well be as follows:

Table 1

Cost centre/Department	Subjective
0509/04	G5010
Hardonby Upper School/Arts Dept	Stationery
Committee/Service/Division	Subjective
E/2/03/00	A1001
Education/Schools/Secondary	Teachers' Salaries

Most systems would accept codes in either format and would be capable of linking a particular cost centre with the relevant division of service, as in the above example. Note that in the second case the fifth and sixth digits are redundant as only the first four digits are required to identify the division of service.

In corporate systems standard subjective codes are invariably used. Thus spending on stationery will always be coded to G5010 whether it is incurred in a school or a fire station. Some systems allow short codes of one or two digits to identify commonly used subjectives and it may be possible to ignore the department code if it is redundant, thereby reducing the overall code length to five digits. The fact remains that corporate financial information systems rely on a fairly complex and rigid coding structure. Moreover, the integrity of the system is totally dependent on the accuracy with which transactions are coded.

There are two other important characteristics of what might be described as traditional FIS coding structures. One is fairly obvious, namely that codes, even short codes, are not 'user-friendly' in the sense that there is generally no obvious link between a code and the objective or subjective category to which it refers. In the above example it makes sense for 'E' to identify education codes but, apart from that, there is nothing in either code to make it easy to recognise or remember. This is not generally a problem for the CFO's staff whose work brings them into regular and frequent contact with the coding structure. However, it may be a problem for staff outside the CFO's department, for many of whom coding bills and vouchers is only a very small part of their duties. Pre-printed coding slips can be used in certain cases to alleviate the problem but there remains a real sense in which non-finance staff are required to operate a coding system which is far more complicated than is necessary for their own requirements. Perhaps the greatest omission of all is that, in all probability, no-one has bothered to explain to them why this is necessary. Even in centralised systems many transactions are coded by staff outside the CFO's department and it can therefore be no surprise to learn that dealing with invalid codes and miscodings is a major task for the CFO's staff. This again points to the need for training.

Another increasing problem is that, in most systems, the coding structure defines rigidly the way in which transactions can be analysed and aggregated, and also the coverage and structure of the reports which the system can produce. Aggregation is achieved by identifying all transactions with a common code or part of code. For example the expenditure to date by a particular cost centre is calculated by aggregating the values of all the transactions in the current accounting period with codes which have the first four digits corresponding to that cost centre. This total can also be analysed by subjective category. Consolidation to provide information for a well-defined group of cost centres, such as all primary schools, is fairly straightforward because a specific range of cost centre codes will have been set aside for primary schools.

What the FIS may well be unable to do without modification is, for example, to generate information which relates only to primary schools eligible by statute for LMS, i.e. those with 200 or more pupils. The problem is that these schools will probably have cost centre codes which are scattered throughout the primary school range and the FIS will not be able to pick them out without an additional identifier. Such problems can be overcome by revising the coding structure but the risks involved in this sort of exercise are obvious. Special enquiry routines can also be written to cope with this situation but such an approach requires specialist assistance and is inefficient in terms of computer processing resources. This rigid structure of analysis and reporting is a major weakness when faced with the demands of devolved financial management.

As well as being inflexible in terms of content, reports from the FIS may well be limited to standard formats. At worst many of the standard formats may be entirely unsuitable for the non-finance manager. At best they may meet the needs of some managers but there will inevitably be others whose requirements cannot be satisfied. We all now understand the importance of presentation in ensuring that management information is utilised. Unfortunately this lesson had not been learned when many existing systems were being designed.

The last, but certainly not least, problem with the traditional corporate FIS approach is the timeliness of information which it provides. The defect lies not so much in the system itself but in how and when it acquires some of the transactions data from its feeder systems. The main problem area is creditor payments. When an establishment manager places an order with a supplier he or she has committed resources from the establishment's budget. By the time the supplies have been received, the invoice has arrived at the establishment, the invoice has been passed for payment and the cheque has been produced to reimburse the supplier, a period of several weeks may have elapsed since the order was raised. During that period FIS reports will give an inaccurate picture of the establishment's budget position because the above transaction will not appear in FIS until shortly before the cheque is produced. This will not be the case, of course, if the FIS has a commitments sub-system for recording transactions at the order stage and if that facility has been used by the establishment manager. A commitments facility is now a standard feature of many systems but experience in our own authority suggests that its use will be patchy; and of course it will be of limited value to any manager who does not have direct terminal access to the FIS.

Our view is that success in devolving financial management will depend on managers having access to financial information which is easily accessible, flexible in scope and content, up-to-date and easy to interpret. Many existing corporate financial information systems may be seriously deficient in some or all of these respects.

The way forward

In view of the above comments it is important for us to make clear at this stage our belief that devolution of financial management does not necessarily mean the total abandonment of the corporate financial information system in favour of decentralised systems to suit local needs. Indeed, as finance managers, we are anxious not to lose sight of the benefits which retaining a corporate approach to financial information will preserve, namely greater efficiency and higher integrity.

There is little doubt that hardware and software technology is now sufficiently advanced to enable a corporate solution to the information needs of devolved financial management. Indeed mainframe packages are already on the market which appear to provide the required flexibility of coding, analysis and reporting. Communications facilities are also available to allow any number of outside establishments to have a direct link with the mainframe and therefore immediate access to the FIS and other corporate financial systems such as payroll and creditor payments.

The problems with following this route include the familiar ones of resources and time. All IT developments cost money, take time and require specialist staff resources to plan and implement but those involving mainframe computers seem to consume inordinate amounts of all three. The time-tables which the Government has set for competitive tendering and local management of schools and colleges are both exacting and strict. There are other, even more immediate calls on IT development resources in many authorities, such as the implementation of the community charge. Against this background, the approach which seems to have most to commend it is to select a suitable software package from an outside software house. This will at least make it possible to contain within acceptable limits both the time scale for implementation and the burden on in-house specialist staff. The most sensible attitude in these circumstances is to recognise that perfection is out of reach but that 90% of the ideal may be reasonably cost effective. It is also important to remember that, if this solution is to be attempted, it remains essential to involve users in evaluating the needs and appraising the available packages.

There is no doubt that concerns over the cost and lead time involved in a central solution can only add to the attractions of a local solution based on increasingly cheap (in relative terms), sophisticated and powerful micro-computer technology. However, it is also fair to suggest that this approach will in any case be more immediately attractive to the end-user for reasons which will range from experience of corporate systems to hearsay from colleagues in other authorities. In some authorities the recent drastic reduction in the service provided by the central mainframe computer as a result of industrial action by key specialist staff can only have damaged further the cause of those arguing for any solution which relies heavily on the mainframe.

There is an entire spectrum of options for achieving what might be described as the local solution. The extremes are:

▽   Local micro-computers linked via a network or dial up facility to the central mainframe. Software provided to download relevant data from the mainframe to spreadsheets or database files. Standard routines provided to analyse data locally and generate reports. Direct access locally to central FIS. Central processing of payroll, creditor payments and income to continue.

▽   Stand-alone micro-computers. Software provided to enable all transactions to be processed and recorded locally, and to enable salary payments and creditor cheques to be generated locally. Local data downloaded periodically onto floppy disks and sent to County/Town Hall to update the central financial database.

The main advantages of the first approach are that it:

▽   retains the efficiency benefits of central processing;
▽   requires limited additional expertise and generates only a limited amount of extra administrative work locally; and
▽   safeguards the integrity of the central FIS.

Its main disadvantages are that:

▽   there may be less local flexibility than with more radical options;
▽   the problem of the delay between orders and invoices is not addressed; and
▽   it is vulnerable to mainframe problems such as slow response or system failure, and to communications problems, particularly if dial-up facilities are used.

The pros and cons of the second approach are a mirror image of the above. Clearly one of the CFO's main concerns must be the extent to which his or her statutory responsibilities can continue to be met. Faced with a local solution of the second type, CFOs will need to:

▽ review their requirements in terms of financial procedures and information. For example does the CFO need to have a full record of all local transactions or merely a running total of overall spending to date?

▽ ensure local managers and staff are given adequate financial training and guidance;

▽ provide clear and comprehensive financial regulations for local managers; and

▽ increase the resources available to carry out internal audit work in the relevant service areas.

Devolving financial management responsibilities to local managers will necessitate a considerable amount of training and guidance whatever approach to financial information development is adopted. However, the more radical local solutions to financial information needs will create a much greater immediate training burden because it will be necessary to provide local staff with the expertise and commitment necessary to ensure that transactions are processed and recorded accurately. One of our principal messages is that the 1990s should see a decentralisation of financial functions such as creditor payments. Whether this and more can be achieved successfully in the two- or three-year time scale required by major initiatives such as LMS remains to be seen.

6 Financial management functions — exchequer

Introduction

In the next three chapters we shall describe in more detail the financial management functions listed in Appendix A. We shall concentrate particularly on those functions where devolution of responsibility or physical decentralisation is already well advanced or is feasible in the short to medium term. For each of these functions, we shall endeavour to explain in straightforward terms:

▽ its objectives and component tasks;
▽ the traditional procedures and problems associated with it.

For the remaining functions we shall confine ourselves to a brief outline of their main purpose and characteristics.

This account will be based entirely on our own experience and so may not reflect the situation in all local authorities. To minimise the risk of inaccuracy and irrelevance, it has been necessary to restrict ourselves to very general comments.

Exchequer functions

1 Payroll

The objectives are fairly straightforward, namely to pay the appropriate staff the correct amounts on the due dates. Achieving this in a large organisation with several thousand staff spread across the entire spectrum of professions, trades and working arrangements is a massive and complex commitment.

There are numerous tasks associated with the payroll function. These include:

▽ dealing with new starters and leavers;
▽ updating payroll records for changes of address, bank details, etc.;
▽ statutory deductions from pay —- income tax and national insurance;
▽ other additions to and deductions from pay, including allowances, superannuation deductions and union subscriptions, attachment of earnings and car loan repayments;
▽ dealing with temporary variations in pay, including overtime and unpaid leave;

▽ generating payment by electronic fund transfer (BACS/BACSTEL), crossed cheques to individuals, banks or building societies, open cheques and cash;
▽ implementing pay awards;
▽ dealing with annual increments;
▽ operating the Statutory Sick Pay (SSP) Scheme;
▽ dealing with maternity leave and pay;
▽ providing payroll information to the Department of Social Security (DSS), Inland Revenue and Department of Education and Science (DES) (for teachers);
▽ passing on deductions from pay to DSS, Inland Revenue, DES, HM Paymaster General, trade unions and other bodies;
▽ initiating third party accident claims whereby compensation for absence from work is claimed from insurers.

    For major services the above tasks may be split between payroll staff in the CFO's department and a staffing section in the service department. However, it is not uncommon for the CFO's staff to handle most or all of the above functions for the vast majority of staff.

    Computerised payroll systems are now almost universal. The basis of most systems is a payroll master record which is established for each employee and contains all the information necessary for the purposes of calculating the basic pay of that individual, dealing with any permanent variations and determining the frequency and method of payment. These records are held in payroll master files with, generally speaking, each category of staff being treated separately. In newer systems payroll details are combined with other personal details in a comprehensive personnel database. This is obviously more efficient because it avoids key information, such as home address and date of birth, having to be held in separate computer files.

    The most common method of updating the payroll master file and dealing with time sheets and temporary variations in pay is by batch input of dual purpose forms which are initiated at the establishment or in the service department and are then submitted for data preparation, having first been checked (possibly on a sample basis) and/or completed by the CFO's payroll staff. Several thousand of these forms may arrive in the CFO's department each month. To cope with the large volume of input, the competing demands on computer processing resources and the absolute necessity to pay people on time, strict deadlines must be followed. There will be a separate time-table of deadlines leading up to each weekly or monthly pay-day.

    Salaries and wages account for well over half of local authority revenue spending. It is therefore essential that there are adequate controls within any local authority payroll system to minimise the risk of loss as a result of error or fraud. Traditional methods of control include:

▽ proper authorisation of variation forms and input documents;
▽ manual checking (on a 100 % or sample basis);
▽ exception reports to identify large, unexplained variations;
▽ control totals for batches and for entire processing runs;
▽ periodic internal audit scrutiny.

    The spread of on-line access to and updating of the central payroll systems from remote establishments will create additional security and control problems. Sophisticated systems to control access to payroll data via terminals and micro-computers have been developed to meet this challenge.

The local authority payroll function is fraught with problems. Many of these stem from the high volume and non-uniformity of the transactions involved. Although the majority of local authority employees are now paid monthly by automatic credit transfer, there are still significant numbers of weekly paid staff and, in many authorities, staff who still prefer to be paid by cheque or in cash. A relatively high proportion of local authority employees work part-time, or on a seasonal or termly basis. In a large local authority there will be more than thirty different national pay agreements which need to be applied.

Given this complexity and the need for the CFO's staff to rely on information supplied by non-finance staff at service and establishment level, there is an obvious need for training and guidance. Unfortunately, the increasing pressure on payroll staff, as turnover amongst local government employees increases and ad hoc local arrangements and agreements proliferate, often means that minimal training is given and that user manuals are left unwritten or out of date. At the same time increasing pressures on management at the local level, not least as a result of devolved financial management, can only compromise further the quality and timeliness of the source information being provided. This is a resource problem but also a management problem, involving an urgent review of priorities and procedures.

2 Creditor payments

Not all organisations pursue the same objectives with respect to the creditor payments function. Particularly for a large organisation, the cash flow implications of reducing the settlement period for invoices by one week are significant. If, as in a medium to large local authority, the average weekly creditors' bill is one million pounds, the interest foregone would be in the region of one hundred thousand pounds per annum at current rates of interest. However, the speed with which a large local authority pays its local suppliers is always a sensitive issue politically. We would guess therefore that the primary objective of most local authorities remains to reimburse suppliers promptly and accurately.

Obtaining supplies and services involves the following sequence of events:
(a) placing an order, verbally or in writing;
(b) receiving the goods;
(c) receiving an invoice or bill for the goods;
(d) paying for the goods received.

All four events may occur simultaneously, as in the case of the purchase of a battery from a local retailer using petty cash. More usually, however, there is a time-lag between each stage in the process. The primary concern of the traditional creditor payments function is to control the operations which link stage (c), the receipt of the invoice, with stage (d), payment for the goods or services received. However, most larger local authorities also have computerised facilities, linked either with the creditors system, or the financial information system (FIS), which allow for a commitment to be entered when an order is placed and for the system to be updated as the new order progresses. Indeed, many authorities have gone much further than this and have developed computerised purchase order systems, either alongside or as an integral part of their creditors systems. This enables a much more integrated and efficient approach to the entire procurement operation and provides more useful and up-to-date management information.

There is also considerable variation among local authorities in the extent to which the procedures following receipt of an invoice have been devolved to service departments and outside establishments. The basic tasks at this stage are:

▽ to ensure that an invoice is valid and correct. This is achieved by a combination of:
  — local certification by an authorised officer to confirm that the specified goods or services have been received and that the invoice has not previously been paid;
  — bill examination — various levels of check are possible and the extent of checking may depend upon the value of the invoice. The CFO's minimum requirements will specify minimum bill examination checks. This task has traditionally been performed centrally but can be done locally, if the resources and expertise are available.

▽ to provide the computer with the information necessary to generate a cheque, particularly the name and address of the supplier and the cheque amount. Usually details of all current suppliers are held in a central computer index with each distinct combination of supplier's name and address being allocated a unique creditor number. The appropriate creditor number is entered on a coding slip attached to the invoice along with the invoice amount(s). This task can be done locally as long as there is direct access to the central index.

▽ to provide basic payment details on the cheque remittance advice so that the recipient can readily identify which account(s) is/are being settled. This is particularly important if the corporate system is designed to combine all payments to a single creditor into one cheque when carrying out a cheque run. The procedure is sometimes known as detailing.

▽ to allocate the invoice amounts to the transactions codes within the FIS. This is already a predominantly local operation with preprinted coding slips being widely employed.

▽ to provide an audit trail so that the progress of particular invoices through the system can be followed retrospectively; the simplest way of achieving this is by allocating a unique number to each invoice. In our authority this is known as a tracer number.

Coding slips are only required where batch processing is still employed. The alternative is direct input, either centrally or locally.

Apart from certification and bill examination, traditional centralised creditor payments systems generally include other control operations. It is still common for creditor cheque listings to be 'called over' against the original invoices before the cheques are actually produced. Decentralised systems rely on various types of check built into the system software. Although such systems may well allow creditor payments to be recorded and initiated locally, in most cases the cheques are produced centrally. However, recent initiatives, particularly local management of schools (LMS), are encouraging even more radical reviews of present arrangements and local cheque books are to be provided to LMS schools in some authorities.

Decentralisation of the creditor payments function is therefore well advanced in many local authorities. The attendant problems are no different from those involved in devolving any other financial management function, namely:

∇   to provide adequate, early and useful information locally;
∇   to develop economic local procedures for carrying out the tasks involved;
∇   to provide adequate training (preferably in advance) and guidance;
∇   to ensure effective financial controls are in place and are applied;
∇   to feed the corporate FIS and ensure local and central databases are reconciled.
∇   to provide an audit trail.

The main problems with the existing centralised systems are the high volume of paper which has to be processed and stored, the inefficiency of long-established computerised systems and the somewhat unwieldy control procedures which are currently operated in some authorities. These combine to increase the throughput time for invoices and to magnify the difficulties that staff faces in dealing with queries from suppliers. The local approach has the potential to avoid most of these problems (although it will still be necessary for invoices to be stored for up to five years to satisfy VAT requirements). This potential will be realised if decentralisation is managed properly and within a sensible timescale.

3 Housing benefits

Assistance with rent and rates is covered by three types of means-tested benefit — rate rebates, rent rebates and rent allowances. These are known collectively as housing benefits. There is a statutory scheme covering each element of housing benefit. The benefit criteria and levels for each scheme are set by government regulation. Local authorities have the discretion to augment any or all of the statutory schemes. Payments in relation to the statutory schemes are covered by a direct government subsidy of 97% (subject to certain exceptions). There is also a separate subsidy for the cost of administering the statutory schemes which is paid as a cash-limited specific grant. Payments and administration costs relating to local schemes do not qualify for subsidy.

In England, the burden of administering housing benefits falls exclusively on district and borough councils all of which are both rating authorities and housing authorities. The main tasks involved are:

∇   identifying and advising potential claimants, sending out and collecting completed claim forms;
∇   assessing entitlement to benefits;
∇   providing benefit to those entitled either through:
    —   reductions in rate bills (rate rebates);
    —   reductions in council house rents (rent rebates);
    —   cheques to private sector tenants (rent allowances);
∇   periodically reviewing the circumstances of claimants and reassessing entitlement in the light of any change;

▽ liaising with the Department of Social Security (many claimants are also in
   receipt of supplementary benefit);
▽ completing housing benefit subsidy claims.

This work obviously involves close liaison with the authority's rates
department and housing department.

There have been periodic major changes in housing benefit arrangements
since the scheme was first introduced in 1982. The detailed information
required by authorities to implement these changes has invariably been
supplied by the Government at the last minute. This has caused massive
problems particularly as quite major modifications to assessment procedures
and computer systems have sometimes been needed.

Following the introduction of the community charge in April 1990, rate
rebates will be replaced by community charge rebates. At the time of writing,
many of the detailed regulations required to implement community charge
rebates are still awaited. Although council house sales and more recent
legislative changes affecting housing will progressively reduce the council
housing stock, the likelihood is that the administrative burden of housing
benefits will increase because of higher rents and a switch from rent rebates to
rent allowances which are more difficult and costly to administer. In addition,
the recently introduced upper limit of 80% on the proportion of rates that can
be rebated will continue under the community charge. Although the
Government has pledged to provide the other 20% via income support in
appropriate cases, there is a distinct possibility that the support will not match
the amount due. This will give rise both to personal hardship and to problems
of collection.

4 Income

Even if the income from housing rents and other council housing activities
is excluded, the total of non-grant income collected by local authorities is
currently around £5,000 million. Collecting and accounting for such a large
sum is a major task. The main objectives here must be the prompt collection,
banking and recording of all income due to the authority.

Much of this income is collected locally in the form of cash or cheques at or
about the time at which the service is provided. Examples are income from
school meals and the use of sports and leisure facilities. Normally the money
collected is paid in at a local bank or post office and credited automatically to
the authority's bank or National Giro account. Vouchers giving the relevant
details have in the past been sent to the CFO's department so that the
transactions can be input to the central FIS and reconciled with the authority's
bank statements. In larger establishments such as FE colleges and leisure
centres, there is an increasing demand for the facility to pay by credit card.
Some authorities are resisting this development because of the added
procedural complexity. However, the pressure for change will eventually
become irresistible and there may be compensating benefits if the availability
of credit card facilities reduces the need for debtor accounts to be raised and
lessens the physical and security problems associated with cash collection.
Increasingly, the transfer of funds between large organisations is being done by
electronic fund transfer (BACS).

The other principal method of income collection is usually referred to as the sundry debtors system and involves raising an account for the services provided. Debtor accounts are usually raised in triplicate. The top copy is handed or sent to the individual or organisation to whom the services have been provided. It will contain guidance on how payment can be made and often will include a detachable slip which can be enclosed with the appropriate remittance. Of the other copies one will be retained by the department or establishment which raised the account. The remaining copy will be sent to the CFO's department to enable the transaction to be input in the computerised sundry debtors system and, via that system, to be fed into the FIS.

The main functions of traditional sundry debtors systems are—

▽   to generate debt recovery action such as reminders automatically at predetermined intervals;
▽   to deal with adjustments to accounts and write-offs;
▽   to cancel the debt when payment is received and to deal with payments by instalments;
▽   to provide management information to facilitate debt recovery. Such information might include outstanding accounts analysed by individual debtor or by age of debt;
▽   to provide indications of performance in relation to debt collection and recovery;
▽   to maintain a record of unallocated receipts — money received which cannot be linked with a specific debt or service provided.

A large number of debtor accounts are raised by the CFO's staff. These are likely to include:

▽   periodic debts such as rents, wayleaves, easements, school boarding fees;
▽   accounts for overpayment of salaries or wages where the individual concerned is no longer in employment.

In many authorities debt recovery is hampered by the fact that the FIS is generally updated at the time debtor account is raised. This means that income is credited to the relevant transaction code before the money is received. This does not provide the department or establishment which raised the account with much of an incentive to chase outstanding debts. As a result debt recovery tends to be given low priority and this serves to increase both the incidence of write-offs and the frequency with which long standing debts have to be referred to the authority's legal department for recovery action through the courts.

Newer systems allow cash/cheque/credit card income and debt collection to be processed locally. Although such systems, if computerised, may well contain sophisticated checks and controls, their ultimate effectiveness probably stems from the fact that a much clearer link exists between the ability to recover a debt and the amount credited as income in the FIS and ultimately in the accounts.

Council house rent collection is a major financial management function of district and borough councils in England. In 1985/86 the gross income from housing rents was over £3,500 million. Apart from the massive scale of the operation, the other traditional characteristic of rent collection has been the personal visit, both by the rent collector to the tenant and by the tenant to the rent office, as a method of payment. However, more up-to-date payment methods such as direct debit are gradually gaining ground.

Council house rent bills are generally inclusive of domestic rates. The interface between the rate collection and rent collection systems has therefore been very important in the past. The introduction of the community charge will sever this link and council house tenants will in future settle their local tax liability separately from their rent bill. This is one of the many areas where the impending changes in local goverment finance (see Appendix B) will impair efficiency. On the other hand, the burden of rent collection on local authorities is being progressively reduced by council house sales and the wholesale transfer of housing stock to the private sector under the 1988 Housing Act.

5 Superannuation

In common with many other areas of local government finance, superannuation administration is currently coming to terms with major new legislation.

In the shire areas superannuation administration is based at county level and it is the County Council's superannuation section which looks after all the superannuable employees of the district or borough councils within the county. In addition to the Local Government Superannuation Scheme which covers most staff, there are separate statutory pension schemes for police and fire brigade staff. It is also necessary for local authority superannuation staff to liaise with the Department of Education and Science (DES) which administers the teachers' superannuation scheme.

The principal tasks of superannuation staff are:

▽ dealing with new admissions to one or other of the schemes (generally employees who have recently joined one of the constituent authorities);
▽ dealing with employees who are moving to authorities outside the area or are leaving local government. This may entail transferring an employee to another superannuation fund or setting up deferred benefit arrangements or, occasionally, a refund of contributions;
▽ calculating and paying benefits to those eligible, including employees made redundant or granted early retirement;
▽ advising staff on superannuation matters in general and particularly on the new options now available to them, namely, additional voluntary contributions (AVCs) and the freedom to opt out;
▽ promoting the local government superannuation scheme.

The final task is new and has arisen as a direct result of government legislation allowing all employees the freedom to make their own pension arrangements. This means that local authority schemes must be marketed in the same way as similar schemes in the private sector.

Our view would be that, given the specialised and complex nature of superannuation administration, this function is likely to remain under the central control of the CFO for the foreseeable future.

6 Non-domestic rate collection

Under the new system of local government finance, domestic rates will be abolished but local authorities will continue to collect rates from business rate payers. In non-urban areas business property represents a small proportion of all property currently under rating in terms of the number of units or hereditaments, but accounts for roughly half of existing rate income. non-domestic rate collection will therefore remain a substantial commitment for district and borough councils.

As described in Appendix B, a uniform national rate will be fixed by Government each year. District and borough councils will then produce and despatch rate bills and be responsible for all aspects of collection and recovery. As before, rateable values will be determined by the Inland Revenue, indeed a revaluation has just been carried out and the new rateable values will be phased in from April 1990.

The amount of business rates collected by a rating authority will not necessarily be the same as the share of non-domestic rate receipts to which it is entitled in order to finance the spending by the local authorities in its area (see Appendix B). Money will need to be transferred either from the Government to the rating authority to supplement the amount collected locally or vice versa, in the event of the local proceeds exceeding the local entitlement.

There are various contentious issues surrounding the new arrangements, some of which have not yet been fully resolved. These include:

▽   how to deal with losses on collection, i.e. amounts not recovered because of non-payment or as a result of charitable relief and relief for empty properties. Such losses will be allowed for in calculating the local contribution to the national pool but the precise details have yet to be finalised.

▽   how to deal with costs of collection — the intention is for these be borne by the collection authority itself rather than being charged to the Community Charge Collection Fund and thus shared between all the authorities in the areas. However, there will be a government contribution towards these costs which will be paid through the community charge collection fund.

▽   transitional arrangements — the effect of measures to phase in the combined effect of the revaluation and the national non-domestic rate may still be felt by some ratepayers in 1995, when the next revaluation is planned.

7 Community charge collection

Domestic rating is a tax on property whereas the community charge is a tax on individuals. This is a very important distinction when it comes to collection because property is static where individuals are not. The replacement of domestic rates by the community charge therefore means that collecting authorities will in future have to contend with a mobile tax base. This suggests that losses on collection as a result of avoidance and evasion will be greater than at present. Initial experience in Scotland, where the community charge was introduced in April 1989, bears this out although some of the worst predictions do not yet seem to have been fulfilled.

Some of the problems associated with the domestic rating system, such as vacant property, second homes and mixed property, i.e. that used for domestic and non-domestic purposes, will carry over into the new system. However, various new difficulties will face collecting authorities, particularly:

▽ keeping up to date the community charge register;
▽ identifying those who become liable for the community charge as a result of reaching the age of eighteen;
▽ identifying and verifying those who are wholly or partly exempt from the charge (see Appendix B);
▽ dealing with the collective community charge which is intended to cover rented accommodation in multiple residence where the turnover of residents is high;
▽ applying the civil penalties which have been specified in the Local Government Finance Act 1988 for failure to register;
▽ dealing with the much larger number of rebates which will arise under the new system.

The basic collection procedures for the community charge will be similar to those required for domestic rates. Community charge bills will be sent out in March/April and similar payment methods will be available, i.e. by post, by personal visit or automatically by direct debit. However, payment by instalment will replace half-yearly payments as the default method. There will in any case be between two and three times as many tax-payers. The scale of the operation will therefore be much greater. There is little or no scope for limiting the additional administrative burden because of the Government's insistence that each individual tax-payer should receive a separate bill, even where there are two or more tax-payers in the same household. This gives rise to the concern that costs of collection will represent a much larger percentage of the amount collected under the new system than is the case with the domestic rating system which, despite its many faults, is relatively efficient in collection terms. Another concern is that there will be cash flow problems for collecting authorities as a result both of higher levels of avoidance and evasion, and of the greatly increased use of instalments.

8 VAT administration

Although local authorities do not, in the main, bear VAT, there must be a system in place to account for all the VAT which an authority has paid to those of its suppliers who are standard-rated. This amount can then be reclaimed from HM Customs & Excise.

In addition certain local authority services, particularly those that are provided in parallel with the private sector, are liable for VAT. Car parking and trade refuse collection are obvious examples. It is essential to ensure that suitable arrangements exist for collecting and accounting for the appropriate amounts of VAT.

The need for VAT expertise within local government is heightened by the recent introduction of penalties for errors in monthly VAT returns. In future errors could lead to a 'serious misdeclaration' surcharge of thirty per cent of the error plus interest. In addition the 1989 Finance Act extends the coverage of VAT to some areas of construction work and to certain transactions involving the sale or letting of land and/or property.

The limited scope and specialist nature of VAT administration, plus the need for VAT returns to be provided on a corporate basis, means there is little point in devolving this particular function outside the CFO's department.

9 Insurance

Local authorities own large amounts of property and equipment. They also employ large numbers of people. Last, and by no means least, they have frequent and regular contact with the general public, both as direct service providers, and as regulatory and advisory bodies.

The wide spectrum of day-to-day activities in which local authorities are involved gives rise to various risks, many of which are insurable. The main categories of risk are:

▽ property — loss, destruction or damage;
▽ liability — the effects of error, omission, fraud or negligence;
▽ motor — death/injury to employees and third parties, plus damage.

There is growing, if belated, recognition in local government that the primary aim should be to minimise risk. Risk management, as this activity is now called, is a responsibility of all local authority managers. However, awareness-raising, training and expert guidance still tend to be left very much to the insurance officer, who is usually based within the CFO's department.

The other tasks of the insurance officer and his or her staff are to:

▽ review periodically the range and level of insurance cover. In a large organisation it may well be a realistic option to do without insurance cover for certain categories of risk;
▽ negotiate with external insurers to obtain the desired cover on the most favourable terms. Most authorities carry out a periodic tendering exercise;
▽ manage the insurance fund, if one exists;
▽ deal with all insurance claims affecting the authority, in consultation with the appropriate service department and, sometimes, the legal department.

By establishing an insurance fund, an authority can exercise a degree of self-insurance. Such a fund is established initially by means of a lump sum contribution from the centre. The fund's resources are then used to meet claims in certain specific risk area, e.g. motor vehicles. The relevant establishments and services are charged premiums for the cover provided and these are paid into the fund. If properly managed, the fund will grow over time and this will enable self-insurance to be expanded. The underlying purpose is to obtain the most cost-effective insurance cover by improving cash flow and avoiding the profit margin applied by external insurers.

As conventional insurance cover becomes increasingly expensive a new approach in larger local authorities is to combine risk management and self-insurance with stop-loss cover. Under this type of arrangement the authority covers all the risks itself unless the losses exceed a given threshold (usually quite high). The threshold may apply to a financial year or to a single event. Alternatively, there may be a separate threshold for each.

Insurance is another financial management function where the advantages of a corporate approach and the degree of expertise required make it difficult to envisage devolution to any significant extent.

7 Financial management functions — co-ordination, control and accountability

1. Financial planning

In recent years it has been very difficult for local authorities to engage in sensible forward planning, mainly because of the financial constraints and uncertainties created by government intervention. The gradual resurgence of strategic planning has come about, not because the situation is becoming easier, but because local authorities are recognising that a flexible business plan with clear objectives, priorities and resource options, is essential to maximise effectiveness. It also reflects:

▽ the growing desire to identify and meet the needs of consumers — this requires both research and planning;
▽ the impact of legislation which is forcing local authorities to devolve detailed managerial responsibility and thus obliging them to confine policy decision to the strategic level.

The preferred outcome of a strategic planning exercise would in our view be:

▽ a prioritised statement of achievable objectives taking account of:
— statutory commitments;
— local needs and circumstances;
— members' policy requirements.
▽ a plan setting out in resource terms how these objectives will be achieved. This should include an allocation of both capital and revenue resources over broad service areas for the period of the plan.
▽ statements indicating the underlying assumptions on which the plan has been based and identifying any factors which cannot be quantified but which may hamper achievement of the plan. Trends in inflation, interest rates and government grant are obvious examples.

A strategic plan is unlikely to be sufficient as it stands for detailed policy implementation. In addition there is a statutory requirement for local authorities to produce annual revenue budgets so that precepts can be levied and levels of local taxation, i.e. rates/community charge, fixed.

Annual revenue budget

Given the financial restrictions and uncertainties which have preoccupied local authorities in recent years, it is not surprising that the annual revenue budget has generally been the predominant vehicle for policy planning and implementation in local authorities.

The annual revenue budget or estimates process is a long-established and reasonably familiar exercise in all local authorities. At one time and in some authorities, the preparation of revenue estimates was an exclusive preserve of the CFO. The norm these days is very much for service departments to prepare the detailed estimates and for the CFO's staff to:

▽   exercise a co-ordinating and advisory role to ensure accuracy and consistency;
▽   deal with areas of the budget which are outside service department control, e.g. support service recharges, capital financing costs, contingencies.

At present local authority annual revenue budgets are statements of resource inputs, possibly supplemented by lists of objectives and statistical comparisons, both between authorities and over time, of service levels and standards. As the 1990s advance, the emphasis will perhaps shift towards target performance levels for each specific activity along with a statement, containing only appropriate detail, of anticipated resource costs. For the moment, however, input budgeting will remain almost universal.

The annual revenue budget can be drawn up in a variety of ways:

▽   zero based;
▽   continuation;
▽   commitment;
▽   cash limited.

It is important for non-finance managers to appreciate how these approaches differ both in their rationale and as to their suitability in practice.

Zero based budgeting (ZBB)

This is a method whereby an entire activity or area of the budget is examined in relation to its objectives and a comprehensive review is undertaken of the full range of available options for achieving those objectives. It is often described as a 'needs-led' or 'root and branch' approach. Theoretically it is the most satisfactory approach to budgeting because it questions every aspect of the activity under scrutiny. However, it is extremely time-consuming and could not be undertaken every year for any of the major local authority services without a substantial input of staff resources, both by the CFO's department and by the relevant service department. An alternative approach, which is currently under consideration in our own authority, is to subject each service to a ZBB review every (say) five years. In the intervening years one of the other budgetary approaches described below would be used.

Continuation (or incremental) budgeting

Continuation budgeting is a widely used system which attempts to identify the

level of spending which would be required in the forward year to continue
existing policies and standards of service provision. An incremental approach
is used in practice with the following adjustments being applied to the current
year or base budget:

▽   full year effects — to take account of policies or changes in activity which
    have been introduced part way through the current year;
▽   once-and-for-all items — one-off items of expenditure or income in the
    current year;
▽   demographic trends — expected changes in client numbers, e.g. school
    pupils;
▽   statutory requirements — the unavoidable impact of new legislation
    which may necessitate additional or reduced spending;
▽   revenue consequences of the capital programme — extra revenue costs
    generated by capital projects, including additional operating costs as well
    as capital financing costs;
▽   inflation — the estimated cost of pay awards, price increases and trends in
    interest rates.

The main advantages of the continuation budget approach are that its
rationale is well understood and accepted, particularly by non-finance
managers, and that it provides a suitable base from which to make policy
changes in either direction. Its problems are those of interpretation and
consistency. There is a host of different ways in which the continuation of
present policies can be interpreted and this leads to both inconsistency and
disagreement, usually between the CFO's staff and service department
managers. One area of recent controversy in our own authority is the extent to
which the withdrawal of central government funding for specific projects can
be allowed for in the continuation budget. This problem stems from the
Government's increasing inclination to 'pump prime' its favoured initiatives
by targeting grant support during the planning and implementation stage
which is subsequently withdrawn, once the initative has been developed.

Commitment budgeting

A voluntary code which has recently been issued on strategic planning and
budgeting recommends a commitment approach to budgeting. A commitment
budget will invariably be less than a continuation budget because the former
will exclude activities which are discretionary in nature. Although this is an
easy enough concept to grasp, it is very difficult to define clearly. Where is the
line to be drawn; to restrict commitment budgets to activities where there is a
clear statutory duty would surely be unduly harsh? Agreed definitions and
boundaries will need to be established at the outset.

Cash-limited budgeting

The essence of this approach is the acceptance that policy planning and
implementation must be finance-led. This is the approach employed by the
Government in managing its own departments and in attempting to control
local authority revenue spending through the grants system. It is conceptually
simple. The forward year's budget for a particular service area is fixed in
volume terms, possibly using one of the other budgeting methods described

above. An allowance is added for anticipated inflation and the service then has to be managed within the overall cash limit. This is an effective procedure for delivering budgets on target but usually makes life more difficult for service managers than the established continuation approach.

To combine strategic planning with a global ZBB approach to the annual revenue budget would appear both wasteful and unworkable. What the 1990s may see is less reliance on the traditional line-by-line continuation budget approach to local authority financial planning and a shift towards —

▽   a medium term strategy covering three or more years;
▽   a two- or three-year capital programme to support this strategy;
▽   a less detailed annual revenue budget geared to the objectives, commitments and priorities identified in the medium term plan;
▽   cash limits combined with wider powers of virement (transfer between budget heads);
▽   increased flexibility between years, e.g. automatic carry forward of unspent budget provision (within specified limits);
▽   performance targets for at least some areas of the budget;
▽   a rolling programme of ZBB or other in-depth service review.

Capital budgeting

Non-finance managers' familiarity with the annual revenue budget process does not usually extend to the area of capital budgeting. There are a number of reasons for this. Capital projects tend to be very expensive and to span more than one year. Major projects often have distinct stages, such as:

▽   feasibility and design;
▽   land acquisition;
▽   site preparation;
▽   construction;
▽   equipment installation;
▽   landscaping.

Each project must be painstakingly planned, and the figures in the capital programme showing the estimated payments flow for a particular project are usually the outcome of a major corporate exercise.

Other characteristics of capital projects are equally important in encouraging a centralised approach to capital budgeting. Principal among these are:

▽   the choice of financing methods;
▽   capital control implications.

These are explained in Appendix C. Limitations on local authority capital spending in recent years have made a corporate approach to capital budgeting essential. It is significant that schemes intended to decentralise decision-making, such as local management of schools, have specifically excluded capital spending from the devolution process.

2 Budgetary control

The preoccupation with resource inputs rather than outputs, the highly centralised structure of most local authorities, and the emphasis on probity and accountability, have all contributed to a conservative approach to budgetary control in local government. Generally speaking budgetary control is and always has been an exercise purely to contain actual expenditure within the budget provided, both in overall terms and at the detailed level.

To facilitate this task budget holders are generally provided with monthly tabulations produced by the financial information system (FIS). These show details of expenditure and income to date for each budget line and compare these with the approved budget. A standard budget monitoring report will have a separate line for each budget head with separate columns showing:

▽ transaction code;
▽ narrative description e.g. caretakers' salaries;
▽ expenditure in current month (and possibly expenditure in one or two previous months as well);
▽ expenditure to date in the current financial year;
▽ approved budget;
▽ variance from budget expressed in both cash and percentage terms.

Some systems are able to display expenditure at the same stage in the previous year and to compare that with out-turn expenditure for the year.

Such reports contain a great deal of information and much of it is very useful. Indeed it is fair to argue that many budget holders do not make the fullest use of their budget monitoring reports. The first step to improving budgetary control may well be to provide budget holders with basic training in how to interpret and utilise these reports.

However, it must also be said that monthly tabulations are often cumbersome, poorly laid out, unduly cluttered with figures and, above all, out of date. Some of the information contained in these reports is probably irrelevant to the budget holder because it relates to budget lines such as repairs to premises, administrative recharges and capital financing costs, over which he or she has no direct control. Moreover, many of these budget lines show nil expenditure until the year end. This distorts comparisons between budget and actual spending to date for the establishment or service as a whole.

As explained in chapter 5, the FIS, and hence the reports produced from it, will not give an up-to-date picture of invoices passed for payment unless a commitments system is available and is used. Another reason why monitoring reports are often out of date by the time they reach budget holders is simply that it takes several days, if not a week, to print, separate and distribute them, particularly in large organisations where month-end tabulations are generated automatically for all budget holders at the same time.

There are several obvious improvements that can be made to this sort of system. These include:

▽ limiting reports to controllable budget heads only;
▽ including commitments, if possible;
▽ reducing the number of columns;
▽ rounding numbers as far as possible to reduce clutter;
▽ highlighting areas of concern, e.g. overspends;
▽ providing exception reports, i.e. only showing budgets which are overspent.

Non-finance managers who have to suffer these shortcomings and have no alternative sources of budgetary control information, such as on-line access, are entitled to complain and press for improvements. Further sophistication is possible. Comparing the current situation with the position at the same stage in the previous year is a very useful and straightforward budgetary control technique which has already been mentioned. Budget profiling is a substantial refinement which is becoming increasingly available. For areas of the budget where there are seasonal fluctuations a non-linear profile of anticipated expenditure through the year is defined and compared with actual spending to date. For example a quarterly budget profile for electricity might be as follows:

	Percentage of year elapsed	Expected percentage of budget spent
June	25	15
September	50	25
December	75	60
March	100	100

In the absence of profiling the electricity budget would normally appear underspent until the very end of the financial year. It is significant that we have consistently referred to budget monitoring reports rather than budgetary control reports. Management information of this sort provides a basis for decision-making but it does not guarantee that management action will take place. It is important therefore not to confuse budget monitoring with budgetary control. The latter can only be effective if appropriate corrective action is taken when the need arises, i.e. when a significant budget variance occurs or appears likely. This may take the form of a budget overspend, but this need not be so. Underspending can undermine an authority's policy objectives and plans every bit as much as overspending.

When budgetary control is viewed in this way, that is, as a process of monitoring, evaluation and action, it becomes an integral part of the management process described in chapter 1. It also brings conventional budgetary control much closer to the process which is likely to replace it in the 1990s, namely performance review. The missing link is the ability to focus on output rather than input.

3 Final accounts

Local authorities have a statutory duty to prepare annual accounts for each financial year. These are subject to audit by an external auditor appointed by the Audit Commission. There are a variety of statutory requirements and codes of practice governing —

▽   the separate statements which have to be produced;
▽   the format and content of these statements;
▽   the time-table and procedures which have to be followed with regard to publication and public scrutiny of the accounts
▽   external audit requirements and procedures.

It is not the purpose of this book to describe in detail the statutory framework within which local authority final accounts are prepared and published. Closing the accounts, the process which culminates in the publication of the final accounts, is a complex technical exercise which is directly linked with the CFO's statutory responsibilties (see chapter 2). Although staff in service departments and establishments inevitably play an important part in the exercise, the role of co-ordinating and consolidating the process is a core financial function.

4 Statutory reports and returns

Statutory financial returns

All local authority departments are involved in compiling and submitting statutory returns and the CFO's department is certainly no exception. The most important statutory financial returns which authorities have to render are:

▽   Return of expenditure and rates (RER) — an annual return produced in March/April which provides detailed information on the authority's annual revenue budget.
▽   Revenue out-turn/capital out-turn (RO/CO) forms — this is also an annual return and is completed during July as part of the closing programme. It records out-turn spending for each service area on both revenue and capital account.
▽   Capital payments return (CPR) — this quarterly return is used by the Treasury to monitor aggregate capital payments and by other government departments to monitor capital spending by each local authority against block spending approvals (see Appendix C).

Significant revisions to the RER form and the capital payments return will be required for 1990/91 to cope with the new arrangements outlined in Appendices B and C. Changes in format and coverage of statutory returns are a recurring problem and make it especially difficult to automate the compilation process.

Annual report

Although the annual report and the statement of accounts (final accounts) are often combined in a single publication, they are separate entities with distinct objectives. Local authority annual reports are produced in accordance with a separate code of practice whose stated objectives are:

▽   to give rate-payers clear information about local government's activities;
▽   to make it easier for electors, rate-payers and other interested parties to make comparisons of and judgments on the performance of their authorities;
▽   to help councillors form judgments about the performance of their own authority.

The code of practice specifies in some detail the information, both financial and non-financial, which should appear in an authority's annual report. There is also a requirement for general statistics on the scale, usage and cost of services, and specific key service indicators (such as cost per pupil) to be included along with comparative figures for previous years and/or other authorities.

There is now a wide variety of annual report formats in local government. An increasingly popular approach is the newspaper format which can be subsidised by advertising and therefore provides an opportunity for the report to be given wide circulation within the authority's area without undue expense. The CFO's staff now play a more limited though important part in producing the annual report.

Rate notices

There is yet another set of statutory regulations governing the information which must accompany rate demands. Most of the required information is financial and is therefore provided by the CFO's staff. Information must be provided both for the rating authority itself and for any major precepting authorities. This can be done either by distributing separate leaflets or by incorporating the required county council figures in the leaflets produced by each district or borough council. Similar leaflets are likely to accompany community charge demands, although in future there will be more information on the demand note itself.

5 Grant claims

As well as being disturbing from the point of view of local autonomy, the increasing resort by central government to specific grants has led to a growth in the burden of grant claims. The work involved may be considerable and is often shared between the CFO's department and the relevant service department.

Although most of the spending information required for the purposes of calculating block grant has in the past been extracted by the Department of Environment from RER and RO forms (see section 4 above), a large variety of demographic and other non-financial data has in the past been used to calculate grant related expenditure assessments (GREAs) for each authority (see Appendix B). Much of these data is also extracted from existing returns — such as Form 11 for school pupils. However, it is important for non-finance managers to be aware of the potential significance of these data and the need for accuracy in compiling them. For example, each secondary school pupil over the age of sixteen is currently worth £2,776 of GREA and block grant.

Under the new system of local government finance, block grant will be replaced by standard spending grant which will be independent of authorities' spending. However, GREAs will remain under the new title of standard spending assessments (SSAs). Although efforts are being made to simplify their calculation, locally generated data will still be required so that the above exhortation remains valid. Lack of attention to detail could be very expensive for your local authority!

6 Cash flow management

Cash flow is the CFO's professional responsibility. In most larger local authorities there is an officer who spends all or a significant part of his or her time liaising with the money market and the banking institutions in order to try

to maximise the day-to-day cash position of the authority. If one examines a
local authority's estimates in some depth, figures will be seen of interest
payable and receivable, which amount to several million pounds per annum.
The cash flow manager's performance is measured by the size of those figures.

Cash flow management works as follows. An estimate is made each day —
or several times in a day on occasions — of whether the authority requires to
borrow money to fund its requirements, or whether there is a cash excess.
Suppose a cash deficiency of £1 million is identified. There are then two issues
to be decided. Firstly, an effort is made to estimate how long the deficiency will
persist, e.g. overnight, a week, a month, more than a month. This presupposes
the authority has cash balance forecasts sufficiently far ahead. Most authorities
have a weekly forecast for a year ahead, and a daily one for a month ahead.

Having established how long the £1 million will be needed — say seven
days — the cash flow manager then enters the market place, by contacting the
authority's money brokers, a city institution which will know where the best
borrowing rates can be obtained. It is also usual to contact a few financial
institutions with whom the authority deals frequently. This may well secure a
better rate and save the expense of brokerage fees. When the best rate is
identified, the deal is made and £1 million is transferred from, say, a building
society to the authority's account at a clearing bank. It is repaid seven days
later.

The opposite happens if there is a surplus of cash. The authority also has a
list of financial institutions or types of institution to which it will lend. Due
care is needed in choosing a borrower. For the sake of prudence and safety it is
not thought worthwhile to risk a very large sum of money for an extra 1/16 % on
the rate of interest with some of the less well-known secondary financial
institutions. Of course, an authority will accept anyone as a lender. The choice
of borrower is at present up to each authority's individual judgment, although
from 1990/91 lending to a non-authorised body will not be allowed.

Recently an argument has been developing as to the desirability of
individual local authority establishments with devolved powers and
responsibilities being allowed to manage their own cash flow.

There are two aspects to cash flow management:

▽   the cash flow effects of management action, e.g. more effective debt
    collection improves cash flow;
▽   the ability to decide how and when to invest and borrow.

In theory both aspects should be devolved because establishment
management should embrace control over as many resources as practicable.
However, the financial benefits of leaving the second element of cash flow
management at the centre are enormous. Not only will the amount of cash to be
invested or borrowed be much more accurately determined, but the
negotiating position will be vastly superior because large sums will be
involved. Our advice, therefore, would be to calculate the costs to the local
authority before devolving this aspect of cash flow management.

7 Debt management

Like cash flow, and very closely related to it, borrowing is also a professional
duty of the CFO. Borrowing embraces the entire spectrum from overnight

borrowing on overdraft from the authority's own bank to a twenty-five year loan from the Public Works Loans Board (PWLB). It is a prime function of a CFO to attempt to create a portfolio or framework of borrowing arrangements which will be to the financial benefit of the local authority.

These few paragraphs cannot do more than touch on what is a highly technical and complex area. It might be worth noting that many large private sector organisations advertise for group or corporate treasurers at rates of pay in excess of most CFOs'. Their duties are very largely cash flow and borrowing, which take up about one per cent of this book!

There are some fundamental principles that CFOs must consider when examining borrowing requirements:

▽   the availability of other internal funds;
▽   the structure of interest rates for different periods of time;
▽   the future trend of interest rates — in the short and longer term;
▽   the fixed and variable instruments that are on the market;
▽   the PWLB conditions and maximum borrowing levels;
▽   the various limits placed by statutory instruments on temporary borrowing and the bills that can be used for this;
▽   the voluntary agreement between local authorities and the Treasury that the average period of borrowing must be at least seven years;
▽   the redemption period for borrowing; it is not in the interest of the authority for all borrowings to mature at the same time in case interest rates are very high then.

As a result of several years' 'creative accounting' in the face of Government spending restrictions, some local authorities have so little flexibility that they are forced into the market to borrow long-term at a time when they may have wished to tread water. However a wide variety of negotiable and fixed forms of borrowing is now available to accommodate almost any needs. New instruments are continually arriving on the market and city-based specialist advisers are necessary to help CFOs understand what is for sale.

8 Financial management functions — audit, commercial, information and advice

1 Audit

1.1 Internal audit

CIPFA have defined internal audit as 'an *independent* appraisal function within an organisation for the *review* of activities as a *service* to all levels of *management*'. The key words have been italicised. Audit is a financially based independent review function and internal audit is a service to management. Those non-finance managers who have only experienced the traditional 'ticking and checking' approach to internal audit may find this difficult to accept but let us hope that they are now in a significant minority.

There is a statutory duty on each local authority CFO to maintain an 'adequate and effective internal audit'. Recognised guidelines exist which spell out this duty in more detail. They require the internal auditor to monitor:

▽ the effectiveness of routine managerial controls;
▽ the custody and security of assets, and
▽ the adequacy of management information.

Clearly it is impossible for a limited number of staff based in the CFO's department to monitor directly and continuously all areas of activity within a large, diverse and dispersed organisation such as a local authority. Internal audit work must therefore be planned. The objectives of internal audit plans are to establish audit priorities and to ensure the effective use of audit resources.

Audit priorities can be assessed by examining two key aspects of all financial systems:

▽ materiality;
▽ risk.

Materiality is easier to measure. For example, a payroll system which processes transactions with an annual value of £100 million is clearly more material than a petty cash account in a small primary school. Assessing risk is more difficult. Where systems-based auditing is used (see below) previous audit findings can be used to identify systems where the risk of a loss occurring is high, but often the auditor has to rely largely on his or her professional expertise and experience. Indices of risk can be combined with materiality, usually expressed as turnover per annum, to give an estimate of the potential loss in each area of activity in a given period. Where the potential loss exceeds a certain benchmark (say £10,000 per year) it may be decided to review the system annually. If the potential loss is less than (say) £500 per year, the system may not be reviewed at all. Other systems will be reviewed at intervals of between one and five years. This enables the audit plan to be drawn up.

Within local government, there are three accepted internal audit approaches.

▽ **Transactions auditing**
This is the most traditional audit approach and is based on the principle that the validity, accuracy and completeness of an organisation's financial transactions can best be confirmed by an examination of the originating or prime documents. In practice, it is the most reliable approach but also the most cumbersome and the work involved can prove boring and routine. It does not encourage initiative and tends to result in internal audit sections requiring large numbers of staff. Nevertheless, some transactions are so important that they will always have to be audited.

▽ **Systems auditing**
This approach arrived in the mid-1970s from North America. It is based on the principle that most financial transactions pass through a system of controls designed to confirm their validity, accuracy and completeness. The controls provide the checks normally carried out by the auditor when performing a transactions audit. It is not necessary therefore to check so many transactions if it can be confirmed that the system contains all the necessary controls and that these are operating correctly.

Once the initial documentation and evaluation of system controls have been completed, this approach requires a much lower level of audit resources than does transactions auditing. However, the initial workload is substantial and requires a high level of expertise. Consequently, the approach is not yet well developed.

▽ **Systems-based auditing**
Fortunately, some organisations did persevere with systems auditing and in the late 1970s developed from it the technique of systems-based auditing which is now used in many organisations in the public and private sectors.

This approach involves the documentation of system controls only (rather than the flow of documents through the system). It —
— introduces the concept of 'key controls';
— enables the internal auditor to rely upon the findings in previous audit reviews when assessing risk areas in the audit planning process;
— considers the inter-relationship of systems;
— requires the auditor to take a wider managerial view of audit findings.
In practice this approach requires a considerable amount of thought and a

fairly low level of detailed checking. It is essentially a risk-based approach
to internal auditing.

Internal audit plans must be flexible. Incidents occur during the period of
the plan which were not foreseen when the plan was produced but which
require immediate audit attention. The obvious example is an incident of
suspected theft or fraud. Audit plans should include a margin for unplanned
audit work but this may well not be sufficient.

The scope for devolving the internal audit function is discussed in chapter
2. The key issue is probably that of independence. However, it must be
recognised that retaining internal audit work entirely within the CFO's
department as a core function may achieve total independence at a high cost in
terms of audit effectiveness as a service to management. Indeed the traditional
view of audit independence is becoming increasingly difficult to sustain as a
result of the rapid pace of development and the resource difficulties which
most local authorities face. This will be a major issue for debate during the
1990s.

1.2 External audit

The Audit Commission for Local Authorities in England and Wales was
established by statute in the early 1980s. The Commission is responsible to the
Government for the audit of local authorities and has complete control over the
appointment of external auditors. Currently local authorities are audited either
by officers of the District Audit Service, the public body which previously had
a near monopoly of local government audit, or by representatives of private
sector accountancy firms. Fees charged to authorities for external audit are
fixed by the Audit Commission after consultation with the local authority
associations.

The principal duty of the external auditor is to express a formal audit
opinion on the statement of accounts. He or she is required to certify that the
statement of accounts 'presents fairly' the financial position of the authority. If
the auditor is not satisfied on any of the matters on which this opinion has to be
based, the audit opinion should be 'qualified'. This rarely happens in practice
because potential criticism is usually resolved by agreement before this stage is
reached. Where there are areas of concern which do not justify qualification
the auditor may make a report in the public interest or include them in a
management letter at the conclusion of the audit.

A major task of the Audit Commission, since its inception, has been the
promotion of value for money (VFM) in local government. The Commission
has carried out and sponsored a variety of VFM studies in particular service
areas and has invariably managed to identify significant potential savings. The
value of some of this work has been undermined by the Government's
eagerness to make immediate global reductions in its spending forecasts and
grant provision on the basis of the Commission's findings.

The other 'enfant terrible' of the Commission is the annual series of Audit
Commission profiles. Each authority receives its own profile, the main
purpose of which is to compare the authority's spending per head of population
with the average for a group of authorities having similar demographic and
social characteristics. Authorities are grouped in accordance with a

classification known as the Shaw classification and each group is commonly referred to as an 'audit family'. For services where more appropriate client numbers than total population are readily available, e.g. school pupils in the education service, these are used. Differences in unit spending from the family average are converted into cash variances for further effect.

The Audit Commission has made a considerable impact on local government during its relatively short life span. Some might argue that it has done more harm than good by making unjustified claims on the basis of superficial investigation and analysis. However, our view is that the work of the Commission has done much to set local authority members and officers thinking along the right lines, i.e. about economy, efficiency and effectiveness, or — in a word — about management.

2 Commercial

2.1 Project appraisal

Project appraisal is very much a corporate technique and the CFO is only one of many participants, but he or she will invariably draw together the results of the appraisal. Strictly speaking, no commitment to incur additional resources in the future should be approved by a local authority without being accompanied by a project appraisal. Such a criterion would cover the entire capital programme. In some local authorities, this is the position. In others, including our own, only the most complex, political or expensive projects can be appraised fully.

A project appraisal should cover, amongst others, the following factors:

▽   objective of project;
▽   method of achieving objective;
▽   what are alternative methods of achievement and why have these been dismissed;
▽   resource costs —
    — financial — capital and revenue (with revenue shown over several forward years);
    — staffing requirements and likely availability;
    — land needs and availability;
    — effects on IT and systems; central accommodation; any other consequences;
▽   benefits —
    — financial, including rates of return if possible;
    — subjective preferably presented in some form of tabular format;
▽   priority index —
    — difficult to achieve, but possible with a corporate approach;
▽   other relevant points —
    — relationship with other services/outside bodies, etc.

Good project appraisals are difficult to accomplish. They are time-consuming to construct and require intelligent and experienced analytical people to prepare them. Over and above the analyst's recommendations, there is a need for very senior or chief officer input and involvement of members, particularly in relation to benefits and a priority index. This latter criterion may seem to be slightly cosmetic, but given that the public sector is always in the situation of having scarce resources, any help to determine priorities must be good.

Cost/benefit analysis has had a checkered career over the years but without the comprehensive and objective approach associated with that technique, project appraisal would be no more than an arithmetical exercise. Decision-makers need the kind of help which cost/benefit analysis can give and it is for the corporate structure, with the CFO playing a major part, to provide it.

We are conscious that these paragraphs only touch the surface of project appraisal and have not discussed the techniques involved. These however could easily form the substance of another book — which we are not volunteering to write.

2.2 Business planning and support

The recent growth of this function is a direct result of the Local Government Act 1988 which led to a time-table for extending compulsory competitive tendering to the catering, refuse collection, vehicle maintenance, grounds maintenance and cleaning activities of local authorities.

In the wake of this legislation those local authorities wishing to give the relevant in-house staff the chance to compete have established direct service organisations (DSOs). As potential contractors, DSOs have had to be given a separate management structure from that of the local authority (the client). The immediate role of the business support teams has been to provide dedicated support and advice to the DSOs, particularly in the following areas:

▽ business planning — forecasting, modelling, financial projections, pricing, cash flow, investment;
▽ financial advice — development of management information and accounting systems, tender evaluation, preparation of tender bids, review of overheads, advice to DSO board;
▽ financial monitoring/control — budgetary control, inflation monitoring, income monitoring, performance review;
▽ preparation of final accounts — closing time-table, trading accounts and flow of funds statements, rates of return, financial statistics, liaison with external auditor.

This list is by no means exhaustive but it gives a fair indication of the expertise which DSO managers must be able to call on if they are to operate successfully. Clearly this expertise must be independent of the financial support provided for the local authority as client.

This account emphasises the financial aspects of business planning and support. There is also a requirement for non-financial support particularly in relation to personnel, property and legal matters. Although in our own authority the business support team is located in the CFO's department, it could equally be sited in a different department or in a separate location altogether, as it is funded by the DSOs and ultimately accountable to the DSO Board.

2.3 Asset management

Asset management is a corporate function with inputs from:

▽ establishments;
▽ service departments; and
▽ specialist departments (e.g. property, personnel, finance, legal).

The degree of specialisation depends upon the nature of the asset, which can be land and buildings, equipment, people (staff), roads, etc.

For convenience, we are limiting this section on asset management to the management of land and buildings and the CFO's role in that process.

The basis of any asset management system is appropriate information and many local authorities now have computerised databases for property which have the capacity of handling common data for a variety of purposes. Corporate access is allowed and the systems can be designed on a modular basis which enhances flexibility. Such systems would include property information, referenced on a geographic basis, with the following details:

▽ address and type of property;
▽ custodian(s);
▽ tenure of land and key review dates;
▽ maintenance information;
▽ building areas — usage and spare capacity;
▽ cleaning areas;
▽ details of fixtures and fittings and moveable equipment, if appropriate;
▽ rent payment, if relevant.

It is clear from this list that property management is primarily concerned with physical characteristics and there is a minimum of financial information. What is increasingly required is information on the economic cost of the property so that assessments can be made from time to time at a macro level on the viability of the property.

CFOs in the past have not kept financial asset records on this basis. Financial information relating to a property has been based purely on how that property was financed and this could be by:

▽ borrowing by external loan, which has to be repaid;
▽ borrowing from internal capital funds, which need not be repaid;
▽ renting;
▽ leasing — finance or operational;
▽ proceeds of capital receipts;
▽ a one-off contribution from the revenue budget.

This information is irrelevant for the purposes of property management and a new form of capital accounting is currently under discussion at national level. One of the objectives of this new approach is to look at each type of asset and assess for it an economic charge (i.e. what it consumes during the accounting period). This charge should appear in the financial accounts, management accounts and individual property records. Let us hope that the asset management function will become more corporate and more effective in the 1990s.

2.4 Value for money

Value for money or VFM, is now familiar enough to most local authority managers to render a detailed explanation of the concept unnecessary. Internal audit staff within the CFO's department should for some time have been shifting the emphasis of their activities from regularity audit to VFM work. External auditors will certainly have been doing so given the considerable effort that the Audit Commission has put into the VFM studies.

It is probable that every local authority has by now carried out its own value for money initiatives either at the corporate or the service level. Special multi-disciplinary teams may have been established to identify areas suitable for VFM review and either to undertake VFM studies or to commission other colleagues or outside consultants to do so. Reports will have been prepared, perhaps containing impressive lists of potential savings. And then...?

The purpose of this seemingly disparaging résumé is not to cast doubt on the merits of VFM initiatives but to emphasise strongly that they are only of lasting value if their recommendations are implemented thoroughly and kept under review. If VFM studies are to be carried out and implemented successfully a number of requirements must be met:

▽ Senior managers from the service area to be studied must be part of the VFM team.
▽ Specialist advice must be available either within the team or from outside to assist in drawing up the terms of reference for the study.
▽ The leader of the VFM team must be of sufficient status to deal on equal terms with any chief officer affected by the study.
▽ Studies should be limited to identifying more efficient and economic ways of providing the existing service. It may become evident during a study that the best solution is to change the nature or level of service provided. At this point the exercise becomes one of policy review rather than VFM and it is vital to recognise when this occurs.

Considerations of this sort have tended to encourage a corporate approach to VFM work. Unfortunately, although corporate studies are often more effective in identifying savings, they are also more difficult to implement than studies which are internal to particular services. Managers affected by but not involved in corporate VFM studies may well not identify with the recommendations and may have little incentive to implement them, particularly if it is decided to use any savings that are realised for corporate purposes. We would certainly not argue that all VFM savings should be retained locally. However, an agreed division of savings may be an effective compromise in those authorities where the corporate ethos is not sufficiently developed to guarantee the whole-hearted commitment of service managers to the corporate good.

Of course, for VFM work to be effective in the long term it must become a routine management function. There is increasing recognition of this and corporate VFM teams are beginning to give way to:

▽ service level VFM programmes designed to cover all activities over a period of three to five years;

▽   centrally imposed targets for VFM savings, e.g. 0.5% of the net revenue
    budget for each service;
▽   performance review — a much broader exercise of which VFM is an
    integral part.

2.5 Investment management

Investment management is very much a function of the CFO — often
personally. London boroughs, county councils and a lead district in each
metropolitan area, have the task of investing the local authority
superannuation fund for their areas. This fund pays out pensions for A, P, T
and C staff and manual workers. It does not cover teachers and FE lecturers,
police or uniformed fire service employees. The sums involved are very large.
Even in a small county like Somerset, £250 million is invested. Large counties
and the lead metropolitan districts account for thousands of millions of
pounds.

There is a considerable amount of discretion these days in investment
management. The Local Government Superannuation Regulations 1986 set
out various parameters, including the fact that local authorities must take
proper advice and act with reasonable care, skill and caution. Some of the
investment principles involved are as follows:

▽   long-term benefits are sought to pay pensions well into the twenty-first
    century;
▽   short-term 'trading' is discouraged. Funds are exempt from tax and too
    much trading could affect this status;
▽   management must be seen to be professional, in terms of both the people
    involved and the degree to which this is a full-time continuous role;
▽   investments should be prudent. Investing a significant proportion of the
    fund in oil exploration or gold prospecting would not be considered
    prudent;
▽   investments should be reasonably diverse. Excessive holdings in
    particular companies or counties or sectors in the market may be outside
    the regulations.

There are of course political stances which the Trustees, a small group of
councillors usually advised by specialists, might decide to take. A refusal to
invest in South Africa is a topical example. It is unlikely, however, that any
stance like this has ever been of sufficient significance to affect the long-term
performance of funds.

Investment management can take a variety of forms and since the 'Big
Bang' in 1986, when the organisation of stock market operations was
revolutionised, the variety has grown significantly. Some current options
include:

▽   single in-house manager;
▽   as above, plus an external manager with 50% of fund 'in competition';
▽   two or more different types of manager 'in competition';
▽   specialist external managers for, say:
    —   gilt-edged securities;
    —   UK equities;
    —   USA;

— Japan;
— Europe;
— other countries;
— property;
— temporary cash investment.

∇ specialist asset allocation managers (i.e. they will determine the proportion of the fund to invest in the categories listed above);
∇ indexation of all or part of fund to track a selected investment index (with the intention of matching the growth or otherwise of the selected market as a whole).

The whole business is fascinating and, of course, very important financially. Actuaries will value the fund every three years in future and the employers' superannuation contribution will be determined by that valuation. If we in Somerset out-perform the 'average' by 1%, that is worth £2 million in a year, or £8 per adult in community charge terms. The relationship is by no means as simple as this in actuarial terms, but the size of the figures is self-evident. We now publish one-year, five-year and ten-year performance figures, and this will only serve to accentuate the relative achievements of different kinds of management and the different financial institutions involved.

3 Information/advice

3.1 Financial advice

The CFO and his or her staff act as financial advisers to three different client groups:

∇ elected members;
∇ senior managers in other departments;
∇ other managers and all staff in outside establishments and service departments.

In terms of staff hours required the last of these represents the greatest commitment. It is also vital to the smooth running of the authority that advice at this level is readily available, sound and consistent. As the pressure on service providers continues to mount, it is increasingly important for the CFO to have sufficient suitably qualified and experienced staff to meet this need. Not surprisingly such staff are becoming increasingly difficult to recruit and retain.

The challenges in providing financial advice to the other client groups are somewhat different. The most important issue is the need for financial advice to be given as or on behalf of:

∇ the responsible financial officer with a statutory corporate duty to ensure 'the proper administration of (the authority's) financial affairs', and
∇ a professional adviser whose fees are paid by a client service or group of services and who should therefore treat the clients' interests as paramount.

There is here a potential conflict between the interest of a particular client service and the corporate interest, and this often poses a dilemma for the CFO or his/her representative in giving advice. Should advice be 'limiting' so as to ensure probity and protect the corporate interest or should it be 'enabling' so as to promote a particular service activity?

It may be argued, with justification, that if the appropriate corporate ethos is well established and if there is a proper corporate strategy, this dilemma should not arise. In practice, neither condition is likely to be fully satisfied. This problem has become particularly evident in our own authority as we have restructured the CFO's department into service-based, rather than functional, divisions. The responsibility of the Divisional Manager to his or her client department is therefore much clearer now than was the case previously. This link will be further reinforced when service level agreements are in place. This emphasises once more the need for an influential core within the CFO's department which has no vested service interest.

3.2 Management information

This topic has been covered at length in chapter 5 and also features in other chapters. It therefore requires no further exposition at this stage.

3.3 Financial training

A recurring theme of this book is the need for adequate financial training if devolution of financial management during the 1990s is to strengthen rather than weaken local government. This training need covers a very wide range of people. Local management of schools (LMS) alone has introduced an urgent requirement in Somerset to train around two thousand school governors, one hundred head teachers, forty bursars, over one hundred clerical staff in schools and a similar number of centrally based support staff. This is a massive commitment which is clearly beyond the resources of the CFO's department. It can only be met by a combination of:

▽   formal training by outside trainers, dedicated LMS staff and CFO's staff;
▽   cascade training — for example, having been given formal training, head teachers act as trainers for their governors and senior staff;
▽   training packages, including videos;
▽   regular meetings and personal visits;
▽   leaflets, circulars and newsheets;
▽   guidance manuals.

The lessons learned from this exercise should enable us to utilise our limited resources to provide more and better financial training in the long term. However, there is no escaping the fact that effective training, whether in-house or not, takes time and/or money. Either way it must be given high priority and proper resources.

3.4 Performance review

Performance review must be an essential element of financial management in the 1990s. It will be required to:

▽ demonstrate that local authorities are achieving their objectives
    effectively, efficiently and economically;
▽ indicate areas of responsibility which are in need of review;
▽ clarify managerial responsibilities within local authorities and assess how
    well they are being achieved.

One of the long-standing obstacles to the development of performance
review has already been referred to. This is the difficulty of identifying
quantifiable output measures for many local authority services. Significant
progress has recently been made in this area, not so much through the
invention of novel performance indicators but rather by sustained efforts,
particularly on the part of CIPFA and the Audit Commission, to consolidate
and structure the mass of information which is available to fuel the
performance review process.
Several categories of performance measure are now available, including:

▽ Unit costs — although this is an input measure it can be useful in assessing
    performance if there is a standard or average with which to compare, e.g.
    cost per primary school pupil;
▽ Output indicators — service volumes possibly expressed per unit of
    resource input, e.g. number of local searches per staff day, or as a ratio of
    the potential demand, e.g. library service members per 1,000 population;
▽ Utilisation rates — the percentage of full capacity at which a service is
    operating, e.g. occupancy percentage of an elderly persons' home;
▽ Service times — the average time taken to perform a particular activity or
    service, e.g. the time taken to process a mandatory student award
    application.

Although none of these indicators provide a thorough indication of output
or effectiveness, they enable useful comparisons to be made either —

▽ over time, or
▽ between authorities, or
▽ against regional, class of authority or national averages or standards.

Particular care should be taken over inter-authority comparisons because
there may be inconsistencies in the way that the relevant statistics have been
measured, analysed and presented. The impact of Audit Commission profile
information has to some extent been undermined by the ease with which major
variances from the audit family average can be attributed to inconsistencies
and anomalies.
Efforts, particularly by CIPFA, to improve comparability, particularly in
sensitive areas such as support services, are an important element in the
development of performance review. The key role which CIPFA and many
individual local authorities play in compiling and publishing detailed service
statistics should be recognised and sustained. It would indeed be ironic if
performance review were to be undermined by a growing reluctance on the
part of local authorities to complete the statistical returns on which most
existing performance indicators are based. This could happen if the quest for
economy in the brave new world goes too far!

9 New approaches to financial management

Key points

▲ *Service level agreements (SLAs) between the CFO's department and service departments or individual establishments will become the norm during the 1990s.*

▲ *SLAs will make explicit the levels and standards of service to be provided by the CFO's department in respect of each function covered by the agreements; they will also set out the associated charges.*

▲ *SLAs will be subject to minimum standards determined by the CFO to fulfil his or her statutory responsibility.*

▲ *Once fully developed and implemented, SLAs will form the basis on which competition for non-core financial services can be introduced.*

Introduction

In this chapter we shall attempt to describe how the process of preparing local authority financial management to meet the requirements of the 1990s can be managed. In particular we shall introduce the idea of service level agreements (SLAs) and discuss what role they can play in launching the new era.

The subsequent discussion builds on the principles established in chapter 2 concerning the role of the CFO and the definition of core financial management functions.

Core functions

Core financial management functions should not be under the direct control of service departments. Indeed individual service departments should have little or no influence on decisions regarding the constitution of the core and the standard at which it operates. What is possible, in theory, is for a local authority, having defined its core functions corporately, to give this work to a firm of financial specialists, as long as there is still a CFO in post. However, we suggest that a local authority would have to be very dissatisfied with the present provision of core services for it to opt for this course of action. We shall therefore proceed on the assumption that core financial management functions as defined in chapter 2 are provided in-house under the direct control of the CFO.

Functions outside the core

The provision of non-core financial management functions is another matter. Here there is scope, as we have already stated, for some or all of the work to be undertaken by individual service departments. Indeed, this already happens to some degree in virtually every local authority.

In theory, there are three distinct choices facing the service manager, namely:

▽ to buy the relevant services from the CFO;
▽ to buy them from an external accountancy, financial services or banking concern;
▽ to provide them in-house, i.e. within the service department or establishment.

Clearly the above options are not mutually exclusive; a combination of all three approaches might well provide the best solution for the service manager.

How will the service manager decide what to do? More specifically, what information will need to be available to allow a sensible decision to be made? In our view the manager will need to know, for each option:

▽ the scope and quality of service available in respect of each financial management function;
▽ the associated costs.

What must also be clear to all those involved are the requirements and standards which the CFO has set in order to ensure that his or her statutory responsibility can be met. These will inevitably affect costs and they may possibly rule out certain options altogether.

In the traditional local authority situation, the CFO is the provider of most non-core financial services, particularly the basic exchequer functions of payroll, creditors and income. The detailed specification of the services being provided will be well known to the CFO's staff but is unlikely to be familiar to anyone outside the CFO's department. Information on costs will almost certainly be confined to an annual recharge to each department or establishment for central support services, within which it may or may not be possible to identify the charge for financial services.

The above scenario hardly provides the service manager with a sound basis for exercising the choice of options described earlier. Service level agreements (SLAs) between the CFO's department and service departments or establishments provide a way forward by bringing together and making explicit the standards of and charges for services being provided. They also, of course, provide a vehicle for the service manager to accept or reject the non-core financial services available from the CFO.

Service level agreements

The structure and content of SLAs is described in Appendix D, which also includes an extract from our own embryonic version. The practical novelties of SLAs should not disguise the important principles involved, which include:

▽ An agreement. This is a cultural revolution for many finance departments, and other central departments as well, for the concept of SLAs is applicable to all. The days of central establishment recharges are numbered in the 1990s. In future, CFOs will have to agree with their customers in advance exactly what service they want and how much it will cost. Any agreement will be subject to minimum standards determined by the CFO, but the customer, or service manager, will otherwise be free to vary his or her detailed requirements. These might involve totally new services, or simply a more or less detailed check than the CFO's staff have previously carried out on certain transactions. The service manager would have to pay for any enhanced requirement. Once an agreement has been made, the service manager knows his or her financial commitment for the period ahead, unless variations are agreed in the interim.

▽ Variations. These should be confined to:
  — pay and prices, although the concept of cash limits may mean that many agreements are at out turn prices;
  — changes in service level at the behest of the service manager, rather than the CFO;
  — unplanned audit work as the result of suspicion of irregularities, etc.;
  — matters outside the direct control of either party to the agreement (e.g. industrial action).

▽ Accountability. At the end of the financial year, the service manager will be charged in accordance with the agreement together with any agreed variations. If the specified quantity of work has not been achieved (e.g. the audit programme has not been fulfilled) then the overall charge will be less. If the quality of work is below specification in the view of the service manager, then a lower charge may also be appropriate but the scale of reduction may be difficult to determine.

If the CFO has not fulfilled his or her contract with a service manager, there are four possible explanations:
  — resources within CFO's department were switched during the year to undertake work for another service manager;
  — the CFO's resources were simply insufficient because of staff vacancies;
  — the amount of work involved was underestimated;
  — the CFO's staff were less productive than planned, due to poor quality, lack of training, excessive turnover, etc.

In the first two cases, the CFO may be able to agree to a reduced charge while still balancing his books, either because another service manager can be charged more or because vacancies have reduced costs. In the latter two examples however, the CFO is likely to incur a deficit in his or her trading account unless a contingency for this eventuality has been built into charges. The CFO's trading account will be debited with all the costs of the CFO's department and will be credited with the charges contained in all the SLAs involving the CFO's department, adjusted for agreed variations.

The bottom line will be a surplus or a deficit. This will provide the ultimate accountability on the performance of the CFO and his or her staff. We discuss how to deal with profits and losses later in the chapter.

▽ Charging. The way charges are structured is critical to the success or otherwise of SLAs. It has to be remembered that the CFO has only a limited number of customers. Private financial advisers/operators have numerous customers and consequently tend to have reasonably simple charging structures, e.g. £X per hour for different levels of staff or £Y per unit processed. Usually they will only give a firm price if the work involved is of predictable and limited duration.

CFOs can operate between two basic extremes in structuring charges. At one extreme everything could be on a marginal cost basis — £X per hour or y pence per unit. Alternatively there could be a fixed price for the whole package, irrespective of the quantity of input. In practice there is likely to be a two part tariff, with a fixed or standing charge and a variable or unit charge, just as there is in gas, electricity and telephone charges. The CFO has to decide what proportion of his overall costs is in the fixed category in the short to medium term and what is clearly marginal and can be dispensed with quickly if the need arises.

A good example of this can be seen in relation to the payment of creditors. Let us assume that the costs of the payments function are as follows:

Table 2

	£ per annum	£ per annum
Financial systems	20,000	
Section head	12,000	
Accommodation	3,000	35,000
Five payments staff		35,000
Gross annual cost		70,000

and that there are expected to be 70,000 invoices processed per annum. The estimated average processing cost is £1 per invoice. The CFO could say to the service manager that the cost of the service will be £1 per invoice processed. If in the event only 56,000 invoices are processed, then income to the CFO will be only £56,000. However, in the short term the CFO can only save the salary of one member of the payments staff as each member can process 14,000 invoices annually. This will lead to a net loss of £7,000. Alternatively, if the CFO charges a fixed fee of £35,000 and 50 pence per invoice processed, then income to the CFO will be £63,000, a loss of only £7,000. That is equal to the potential saving in staff costs.

It can be seen therefore that the way charges are structured is very important to the viability of the CFO's trading account. There will have to be considerable experimentation in the early years of SLAs until practical experience demonstrates the best way to structure charges.

▽ Arbitration. Those of you who have read the draft SLA in Appendix D may have noticed a provision for the County Secretary and Solicitor to determine disputes arising from the agreement. It will, of course, be a pity if relationships between the CFO and the service manager reach the point at which a third party has to intervene and, indeed, it is hoped that this situation rarely arises.

What has not been addressed is how and by whom disputes arising from the quality of a service are resolved. In financial circles we all have our own ideas about the quality of consultants' reports and the work of external auditors. Some are excellent, others we believe are less than average. Judgments are qualitative and difficult to define. Standards to measure against are difficult to find. This an an area to which CFOs and service management must give serious attention in the future. Performance standards can and should be contained in service level agreements wherever possible. Examples are:

—   to pay creditors correctly within X days of the receipt of the invoice;
—   to collect at least 99% of all income within X weeks of receiving an account;
—   to pay at least 99.5% of employees correctly on the due date.

Penalties could be included in the SLA when performance is outside the agreed parameters. This may be easier said than done because in a complex situation with different departments/establishments participating in a single transaction, it is not easy to apportion blame. Nevertheless if true accountability is to be achieved, solutions will have to be found.

What is much more difficult to define is how to monitor the quality of financial advice, audit work, value for money reports and general provision of financial information. Moreover, with the greatest of respect to County Solicitors, we doubt whether they could adjudicate on such matters. If serious arguments develop in these areas, there must be a very basic doubt about the viability of future relationships. In these circumstances a useful mediator could be the external auditor, although he or she would possibly disagree!

Competition

Service level agreements should:

▽   bring a much higher level of clarity and accountability into the relationship between the CFO and the service manager
▽   encourage competition in the provision of financial services at some stage in the future.

It is this second aspect that now needs to be examined.

At present there is no statutory competition for financial services. In the future there might be. Competition could cover all aspects that have been discussed in this chapter, even the core service, although that is neither likely nor desirable. It may be limited to internal audit provision only, or the exchequer functions only. It may never arise.

Nevertheless, it is important that every local authority seeks to maximise effectiveness and efficiency in the provision of non-core financial management functions and, in our opinion, that means organising them as if competition could occur. Our thoughts on future organisation are contained in the next chapter. Our immediate concern is to establish how to manage the introduction of SLAs to achieve a situation where competition is sustainable in practice and clearly beneficial to the service manager.

It is only fair and reasonable that the CFO should be allowed sufficient time to prepare for competition. This suggests that the concept of SLAs should be allowed to work through from an experimental stage to a firm base for tendering. A suitable programme might be as follows:

▽ Year 1 SLAs are produced for the first time — largely based on estimated figures of time spent on various functions with estimated allocations of cost to those functions. The budget remains under the direct control of the CFO but a shadow trading account is prepared.

▽ Year 2 SLAs are produced with more meaningful figures of service standards, volumes and costs. The budget for financial management functions should now be allocated to the service departments in accordance with the SLAs. Service managers are not allowed to vire any budgetary provision to other expenditure heads without the express approval of the CFO. The CFO's trading account is debited with actual costs and credited with the budget allocations after any agreed virements.

▽ Year 3 As for year 2 but the service manager is allowed to retain all, or a proportion, of savings realised through the SLA, provided that minimum financial standards are attained. The trading account is credited with the actual income due under the charges agreed in the SLA.

▽ Year 4 The service manager may be allowed to seek tenders from other providers of financial services and retain some or all of any consequential savings.

A four-year programme to reach a state of preparedness for competition might seem to be too long. For some CFOs it will certainly be; for others, four years will seem to be not nearly long enough. The extent to which the service department is allowed to retain some or all of the savings is a policy matter. If savings are to be shared, the other main beneficiaries should be the community charge payer and future consumers of the CFO's financial services. The latter objective can be achieved by ploughing savings back to improve financial systems for the future.

Another reason for taking a reasonable time to reach the stage in Year 4 above is that there may be several organisational changes which are appropriate before reaching that position. We consider that staff should be given the best opportunity of retaining the financial work in house. Therefore it will be necessary to examine each financial management function at:

▽ CFO department level;
▽ service department level;
▽ establishment level;

To ensure that overall costs for the provision of financial services are minimised. This examination could well mean that there will be more than one organisational change during this period.

Lastly, we should briefly mention the types of competition that might emerge. We do not intend to approach this aspect in a comprehensive manner as the future might prove us wrong! We shall simply note some of the alternatives which may be available.

One of the key decisions to be made would be how to package the 'contracts'. There is a wide range of options with a single contract for the totality of financial management functions at one extreme and a series of separate contracts for each function at the other. A further possibility would be a contract based on a series of establishments (on a geographical or service basis). The permutations are endless.

The competition which emerges could also take a variety of forms, such as:

▽   the CFO and/or service manager submitting in-house tenders. Depending on the organisation, the in-house tenders could be establishment based;
▽   local or national firms of accountants for some or all of the work;
▽   various bureaux which specialise in exchequer work;
▽   banks or other financial institutions;
▽   computer companies for the provision of operations/development work and possibly other financial services;
▽   a management 'buy-out' which could be through a separately created company, independent of the local authority.

Such a process might be imposed or voluntary.

We shall see many experiments in the months and years ahead. A few local authorities have already committed themselves to some sort of competition and we shall follow their progress with intense interest. The very fact that many local authorities are voluntarily considering such major changes in the way they operate and in the delivery of their central services, is both a tribute to their foresight and a reflection of their continued commitment to effective, efficient and economic local government in the future.

10 Meeting the challenge of the 1990s

Key points

▲ The 1990s will see most non-core financial management functions devolved to service departments and individual establishments.
▲ The CFO's department will contract to between 20 and 30 % of its present size in staffing terms.
▲ The number of finance managers and support staff outside the CFO's department will increase.
▲ In a devolved situation it will be very important to provide proper career development and promotion opportunities for finance staff in order to attract and retain them.
▲ In restructuring financial management functions local authorities should take account of their vulnerability to industrial action.
▲ Performance review will play a key role in achieving effective, efficient and economic delivery of local services in the 1990s.

Introduction

Those of you who have read all of the previous chapters will not be surprised at the conclusion we are about to reach. We have nailed our colours to the mast of accountable management at the lowest practical level. In our view, the days of large centralised finance departments are numbered. In future the dozens or hundreds of individual establishments in each local authority will become totally accountable centres. These include leisure centres, schools, residential establishments, housing area offices, police divisions and fire stations.

The objective of this concluding chapter is to speculate on the kind of financial framework that might be the norm in the 1990s. In arriving at the appropriate framework for each local authority, it would be ideal to use a cost/benefit approach to evaluate alternative options, but not all relevant factors are capable of quantitive measurement. Possibly the best approach is therefore to look at different forms of organisation and assess them against predetermined objectives. These objectives might be to:

▽ minimise the cost of financial management functions in order to allow the maximum resources to be deployed directly in additional service provision for the benefit of the client;

▽   attain the minimum standards determined by the CFO;
▽   achieve the quality and performance standards required by the client;
▽   deliver accurate, relevant, intelligible and timely financial information
     and advice to all levels of management;
▽   ensure the development of a career pattern for those involved in financial
     management.

This last objective is one we have not yet discussed, but it is of critical importance in ensuring the recruitment and retention of high-quality finance managers.

The following is a succinct attempt to describe how the financial management of a large local authority might look in 1995 and then to discuss some of the resulting implications.

CFO's department

We outlined in chapter 2 the core functions which, in our view, should always remain at the centre. They are basically concerned with standard setting, monitoring the quality of financial processing and co-ordinating financial information for the benefit of the local authority. The core will also handle specialist services where it is uneconomical to decentralise and will provide financial training in certain areas. The size of the CFO's department might be between 20 and 30 % of present numbers.

The service department

It is not easy to be specific about the financial management role of the service department in the future. It may act as a filter for the co-ordination of information being passed through to the CFO's department. It may act as a support to establishments when they are in difficulties with technical matters or simply short-staffed. It will perform a monitoring and advisory role, and act as 'auditor' in relation to most of the functions carried out by the establishments. Some of this work will be undertaken by the transfer of CFO's staff, some by existing staff. It is envisaged that ultimately, perhaps by 1995, the exchequer functions, payroll, payment of creditors and collection of income, will be handled primarily by individual establishments. Clearly, however, there will have to be a central facility and a 'control' presence at departmental level. Although the overall number of support staff in service departments will probably decrease during the 1990s; the number employed on financial management functions may remain reasonably stable, or possibly increase.

The establishments

Numbers of finance managers and support staff will certainly grow at this level. The local burden of providing financial information for the purposes of the establishment itself and also for the centre will be much greater than now. The volume of exchequer processing will be significantly greater. Exactly how this will be managed will depend upon several factors. These include:

▽ the size of the establishment — the larger it is, the greater the possibility of attracting specialist staff and being able to afford them;

▽ the location of the establishment — if in an urban area it may be convenient to rely on the central service department for support. If in a rural location, there may be geographically based teams of specialists, including non-finance specialists, to serve all establishments in that area, irrespective of the type of service provision. The availability and cost of IT will be a key factor here;

▽ the role of the establishment — in financial terms a small further education college could be much more complex to manage than a large secondary school.

Financial services DSOs

One significant alternative to this devolution model which some local authorities are considering is a financial services organisation based on competition principles. Under this scenario, the central provision of core functions would remain as we have already described. However, non-core financial services would be operated by a free-standing DSO. This organisation would not come under the control of service managers but would tender to provide financial services to them. It would encompass much of the existing work of the CFO's department and also significant parts of the financial administration at present within service departments. The CFO would, as before, specify minimum financial standards.

This approach is similar to the one that we have advocated in that it provides the service manager with choice in acquiring financial management services. However it is significantly different in structural and procedural terms. The existence of such distinct alternatives at this early stage in the game suggests that there will be a variety of operating frameworks for financial services within local government by the end of the 1990s.

Management information

One of the objectives we defined previously was to deliver accurate, relevant, intelligible and timely information to all levels of management. Information will be the key to successful management in the future and the means of providing it will be a constant source of concern. Most local authorities have large corporate financial data bases. These are an efficient way of delivering information, but the format and content of reports is determined at the centre, rather than at the establishment. Whilst cheap to produce, the information may not possess all the above attributes, and because it is part of a large corporate financial system, changes may well be difficult. Chapter 5 discusses the issues in greater detail.

The reason for stressing this matter again here is that unless useful and intelligible information can be supplied to managers, the objectives of the establishment may not be achieved. If the structure of financial services is geared to an inflexible financial information system, then it is unlikely that economies will result from reorganising the structure. Flexible information systems which can interface simply with the corporate database and meet the demands of the centre must be provided. Some are in position now. By 1995, this should not be a problem, but there will be many trials and tribulations on the way.

Management development

The final objective we stipulated in the introduction to this chapter was the development of a career pattern for those involved in financial management. At the present time one of the major worries of every CFO is how he or she is going to staff the financial management functions in the next few years with people sufficiently well qualified and experienced to operate effectively. Financial training in the public sector is generally of a high standard. CIPFA's education and training arrangements are good, and accountants emerging from the system today are well equipped and therefore keenly sought after, particularly by the private sector. We therefore have a twofold task:

▽   to improve still further professional education and training arrangements, at both pre- and post-qualification stages;
▽   to retain finance staff in local authorities by offering suitable terms and conditions of employment, but also, and especially, job satisfaction and motivation.

It is not the role of this book to begin a detailed discussion into education and training arrangements and terms and conditions of service. What we are keen to do, however, is to put down a few markers as to how we feel these aspects should develop over the next few years. It is for others to further them, as CIPFA is already doing. Some matters requiring attention are:

▽   the need to eliminate the term 'accountant' and to replace it with 'finance manager'. The increasing emphasis on management training in the CIPFA professional syllabus is helpful. Perhaps the suggested amalgamation of CIPFA with the Institute of Chartered Accountants provides a good peg on which to hang this issue;
▽   the need for early recognition that at least 50 % of the work presently carried out by fully qualified accountants can be done by unqualified or partly qualified staff;
▽   the need for service managers to allow and even encourage finance-based staff to comment, discuss and make suggestions in any area pertaining to service provision;
▽   the importance of ensuring that the finance manager is a member of the management team at every organisational level;
▽   the need to encourage finance-based staff to apply for general management

posts, including those of departmental service managers and establishment heads.

We firmly believe that the image of accountants as narrow minded and unimaginative has to be dispelled. Training facilities to encourage the development of managerial skills should therefore be a priority in future. Equally it is not a matter of training people just to provide the CFO's core function, but to cover the whole range of financial management functions. In the medium and long term the benchmark of success will be the extent to which financially trained personnel become service managers and heads of large establishments.

The reason we have spelt out this argument is because job satisfaction is a major factor in retaining staff. If visions and ambitions widen, then interest is likewise extended. The public sector has a head start in terms of job satisfaction, which is the reason most people joined. Developments in the 1990s should encourage this aspect with management skills having to be extended to achieve total resource management, quite a change from the situation we have today.

Industrial action

Recent events prompt us to wonder how the future framework of financial management portrayed here will be affected by industrial action. We have just had to deal with such a situation, in which a minority of financial (including computer) personnel went on strike and managed effectively to halt the operation of the mainframe computer, causing considerable disruption within the CFO's department and elsewhere.

The basic question is whether devolution of financial management functions increases vulnerability to industrial action or otherwise. There has been insufficient opportunity to review this issue and reach even a provisional judgment, but clearly it is a matter which local authorities ought to consider when determining their future organisational structures. The kinds of issue that must be addressed are:

▽ the availability of alternative methods of provision, particularly in key areas such as computer operations;
▽ the implications of having small groups of key workers who may be targeted to achieve maximum disruption;
▽ the need to increase 'insurance' arrangements by duplicating certain key functions;
▽ the effects of and safeguards against long-term disputes.

Performance review

Last but by no means least, we return belatedly to the issue of performance review. It is not wholly inappropriate to mention performance review at this late stage because its proper place is at the end of the cycle. We have already referred to performance review in chapters 1 and 8, but we feel it important to reiterate that it will play a key role in future in achieving the effective, efficient and economic delivery of services.

As we have already pointed out, performance review in the local government context is a difficult process, not least because of the qualitative nature of many of the outputs and the general lack of profit motive. However, with the much sharper definition of objectives and standards of performance which will emerge as accountable management is defined at establishment level, there is a real opportunity to make significant inroads into performance measurement.

Every level of management must be involved in this process and performance measures will be defined for the CFO, departmental service managers and establishment heads. The CFO, in particular, will be involved in helping to measure the performance of many others. Indeed, all financial personnel will have to receive training in this area.

Finally, our last forecast for the 1990s is that, as a result of a much more effective performance measurement process, we shall see significant numbers of staff participating in performance-related pay schemes. Properly designed and applied, these will serve to stimulate motivation and enhance job satisfaction, and local government will thrive. Inadequately designed and insensitively applied, the reverse will happen and local government may not achieve another decade of service, let alone another century!

Appendix A: Summary of financial management functions

1 Exchequer

1.1 Payroll

Salaries, wages, taxable expenses, superannuation contributions, income tax, national insurance, pay awards, increments, sick pay, maternity pay

1.2 Creditor payments

Invoices, non-taxable expenses, grants, awards.

1.3 Housing benefits

Rate rebates, rent rebates and rent allowances

1.4 Income

Housing rents and other income (cash and credit).

1.5 Superannuation

Pension fund administration and payments to former employees

1.6 Non-domestic rate collection
1.7 Community charge collection
1.8 VAT administration
1.9 Insurance

Claims, premiums and Insurance Fund

2 Co-ordination/control/accountability

2.1 Financial planning

Medium term strategy, annual revenue and capital budgets

2.2 Budgetary control

Monitoring, reporting and corrective action where necessary (revenue and capital)

2.3 Final accounts
2.4 Statutory reports and returns

Including annual report

2.5 Grant claims
2.6 Cash flow management
2.7 Debt management

Including leasing and other financing arrangements

3 Audit

3.1 Internal audit
3.2 External audit

4 Commercial

4.1 Project appraisal

Particularly capital programme

4.2 Business planning and support
4.3 Asset management
4.4 Value for money
4.5 Investment management

Particularly superannuation fund investments

5 Information/advice

5.1 Financial advice
5.2 Management information
5.3 Financial training
5.4 Performance review

Appendix B: The financing of local government

Introduction

Local authorities derive their revenue from:

▽ fees and charges for services provided (including housing rents);
▽ government grants;
▽ local taxation — currently rates.

In broad terms around 20 % of local authority revenue spending is covered by fees, charges and non-grant service income. The normal convention when looking at local authority spending is to concentrate on net revenue expenditure, which is gross revenue spending less income from fees and charges.

On this basis aggregate local authority net revenue expenditure in England during l989/90 will be about £34,000 million. Nearly £14,000 million of this (41 %) will be covered by grants from central government. The remainder (59 %) will be met from rates. Rates are a local tax on property; they are levied by rating authorities (district and borough councils) on domestic, industrial and commercial property.

The Local Government Finance Act 1988 introduces a new system of funding for local government services. In England and Wales the new system will start operating on 1 April 1990, one year after its implementation in Scotland. Its main reforms will be:

▽ to introduce a uniform national non-domestic rate for businesses, which will increase from year to year by no more than the change in the retail prices index (RPI);
▽ to employ a simplified system of paying central government grants to local authorities;
▽ to abolish domestic rates and introduce a community charge on persons aged eighteen and over. This is commonly known as the poll tax.

In the remainder of this Appendix we shall describe briefly the way in which the existing system works and how the new system will differ from it. The figures used in this commentary are intended merely to illustrate the orders of magnitude involved; they should not be regarded as projections. Readers should also note that this entire Appendix deals exclusively with revenue expenditure; capital spending is dealt with in Appendix C.

The existing system

Under the present rating system, the rate bill for a particular site, which can be anything from a house and garden to a quarry, depends on the rateable value of the site and the rate poundage set by the local rating authority. Prior to the start of the financial year, each rating authority fixes a rate poundage (expressed as so many pence in the pound). When this poundage is applied to the aggregate rateable value of properties in the district, it will generate sufficient rates income to cover the authority's own spending needs, after allowing for government grants, and precepts by other bodies, usually county and parish councils. The same rate poundage is applied to all property in a rating district but, where a site or hereditament is used partly or wholly for domestic purposes, a discount of up to 18 pence in the pound is allowed. Rating authorities are fully compensated by central government for the resulting loss of rate income by way of domestic rate relief grant.

At present there are two other principal categories of government grant to local authorities — specific grants and block grant. As their name implies, specific grants are paid, often on a simple percentage basis, to support particular areas of local service provision. Current examples include police grant, housing improvement grants and education support grants. Block grant on the other hand, is paid to support local authority spending in general.

Although we are both painfully aware of the machinations of the block grant system, we shall not attempt to explain how it works. Suffice to say that at present the system is extremely complicated, continuously changing and sometimes perverse in its effects. These characteristics do little to enhance local accountability because the link between local spending levels and local rate levels is often blurred by seemingly arbitrary variations in block grant.

As a prelude to introducing the new system of local government finance, four crucial aspects of the current block grant system need to be emphasised:

(a) All county and district councils, as well as metropolitan joint boards, the London Fire and Civil Defence Authority, the Inner London Education Authority and the Metropolitan Police, are eligible to receive block grant.

(b) Block grant is calculated by reference to a needs assessment called the grant-related expenditure assessment (GREA). In order to accomplish (a) above there must a separate GREA for each individual authority. Until now this has been achieved by giving virtually every local authority service its own GRE formula. In practice this means that between 70 and 140 separate items of demographic or other data are needed to calculate an authority's GREA. As there are over 400 local authorities this adds up to over 30,000 data items in all. Hence, the GREA system is rightly criticised as complex and over elaborate.

(c) Until recently an authority's block grant entitlement within a given year was dependent on its actual level of spending and on the level of spending by every other authority. This feature of block grant added considerably to the complexity and uncertainty of the system and has been abandoned for 1988/89 (retrospectively) and 1989/90 as a result of the Rate Support Grants Act 1988.

(d) A well established but thoroughly discredited aspect of the block grant system is safety netting, whereby grant losses for individual authorities

between one year and the next are kept within certain pre-determined limits. Since 1985 grant limitation arrangements, as safety netting has come to be called, have become ever more complicated and contentious as the Government has striven —
— to distinguish between the many different factors which cause grant loss between years in operating safety nets;
— to limit excessive grant gains as well as excessive grant losses;
— to cope with the grant consequences of changes in local government structure, particularly the abolition of the Greater London Council and metropolitan county councils.
Finally in this section, Figure B1 is a much simplified diagrammatic representation of the existing system. It shows the amount of budgeted revenue spending by local authorities in a rural shire county during the 1989/90

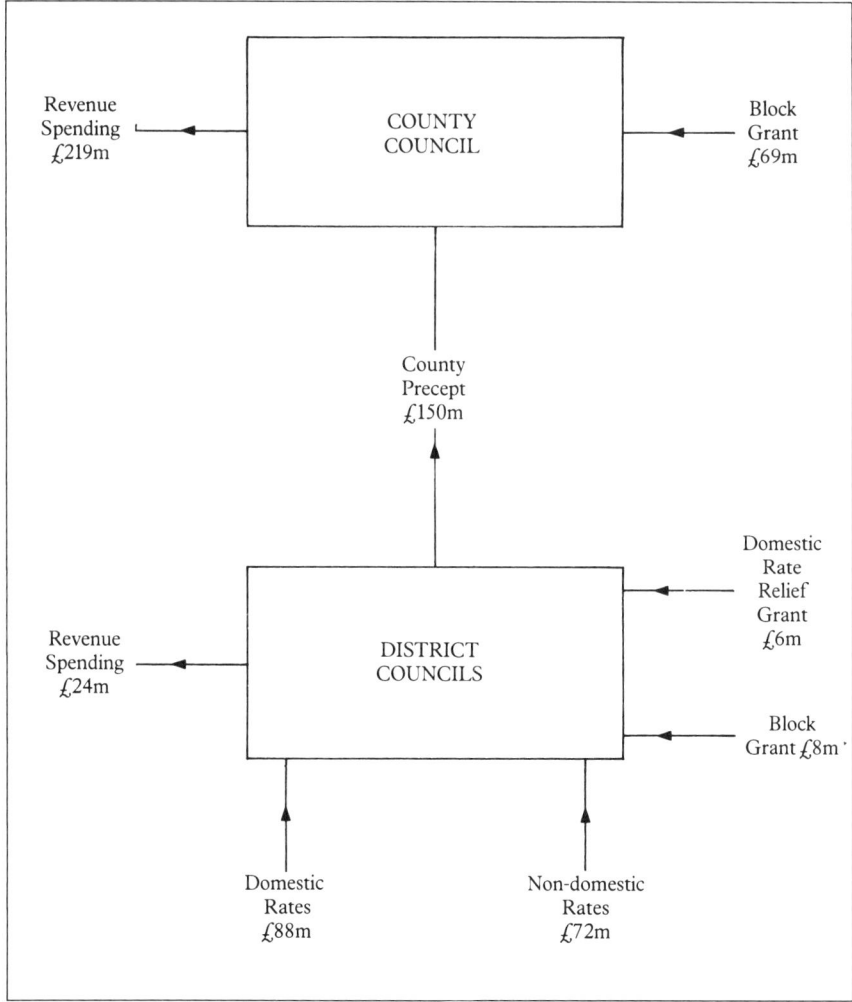

Figure B1 – Present system of Local Government Finance

financial year and how this will be financed. In interpreting these illustrative figures, it should be noted that:

▽   As well as being net of income from fees and charges, revenue spending is
     net of specific government grants.
▽   At district level revenue spending refers to rate fund revenue expenditure
     and conceals a considerably higher level of gross expenditure which is
     offset by substantial income.
▽   District spending includes about £1 million of precepts by parish councils.

We hope that this diagram makes clear that the County precept on the district councils is net of the County Council's £69 million block grant receipt, that the total of rate support grant received by the local authorities in 1989/90 will be around £83 million, and that the combination of domestic and non-domestic rates will generate £160 million. Thus an independent source of local revenue i.e. rates, will cover over 65 % of net revenue spending by these local authorities.

The description of rates as an 'independent' source of local revenue will doubtless have raised a few hackles, particularly among those readers who are associated with rate-capped authorities. Rate capping represents the Government's ultimate sanction against individual local authorities who are deemed to be overspending. It is a powerful and direct restriction on local autonomy. The fact that the new system will contain similar powers is an indication that the Government is leaving nothing to chance in its mission to control local authority spending.

The new system

Government disenchantment with the existing system of local government finance culminated in the publication in 1986 of a Green Paper entitled 'Paying for Local Government'. The Green Paper catalogued the shortcomings of the system with particular emphasis being placed on problems with local accountability, namely:

·▽   the absence of a business vote despite the fact that non-domestic rates
     account for roughly half of local authority rate income;
▽   the fact that, of the 35 million local electors in England, only the 18 million
     householders pay rates and, because of rate rebates, only 12 million pay
     rates in full;
▽   the complexity and instability of the grants system and the consequential
     distortion of the link between local spending and local rate levels.

To remedy these shortcomings the Green Paper put forward the three major reforms listed in the introduction to this Appendix. In the face of considerable but fragmented hostility from the local authority side, the original package remained intact and was eventually enacted in the 1988 Act. We shall now look at each element in turn.

Non-domestic rates

From April 1990 a uniform national non-domestic rate will be levied throughout England. The rate levy will be fixed by central Government at the start of each financial year and the year-on-year increase will be not more than the increase in the retail prices index (RPI) for the year up to the preceding September.

The proceeds of the national non-domestic rate levy will be treated as a national pool which will be redistributed to the collection funds to be administered by each district and borough council on the basis of a fixed amount per adult.

The effect of this reform is illustrated in Figure B2. Under the present system whereby the non-domestic rate levy is fixed locally, rate levies vary between 122.2 and 400.3 pence in the pound and the proceeds are retained locally. Under the new system a national non-domestic rate levy of 261.6 pence

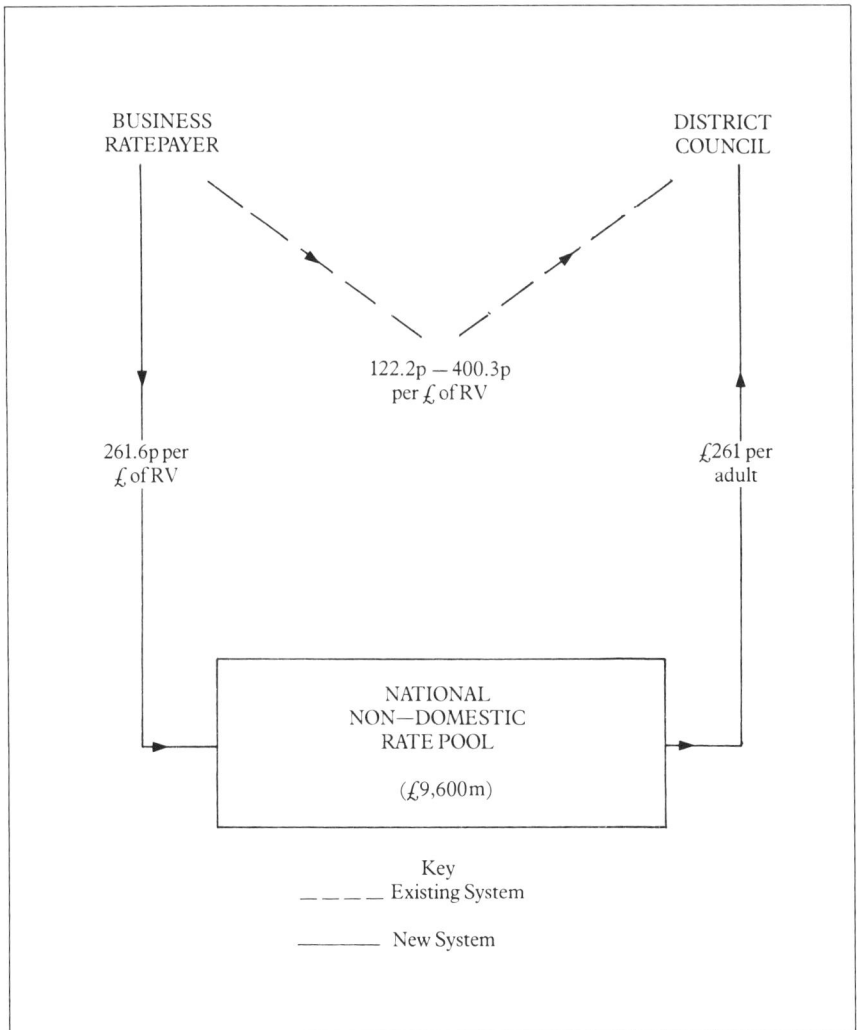

Figure B2 – Non-domestic rate, *England 1989/90*

in the pound would be needed to generate an equivalent amount of rate income. This would be pooled and redistributed as £261 per adult to each district collection fund. Readers should note that the closeness of these two figures is entirely coincidental.

Clearly the move to the new system will affect both the amount that is paid by most non-domestic ratepayers and the amount that each district council receives in respect of non-domestic rates. In our typical shire county, for example, the 1989/90 rate bill for local businesses would have been slightly lower but the total non-domestic rate income for the county area, at £90 million, would have been £19 million more than the amount collected locally.

Two other points must be made about non-domestic rates. Firstly, it must be recognised that over time the new system will lead to a decline nationally in the relative contribution which non-domestic rates make to local authority funding unless:

▽ the year-on-year increase in the national non-domestic rate matches the RPI increase in full, and;
▽ the year-on-year growth in local authority spending does not exceed the increase in RPI.

Otherwise there will be a relative increase in the community charge burden unless higher levels of government grant are used to bridge the gap, which seems unlikely.

Secondly the entire situation is complicated by the decision to carry out a non-domestic rating revaluation and to introduce the new rateable values at the same time as the new system is implemented. At the time of writing it appears that rateable values will increase by a factor of about 7 or 8, which means that the actual national non-domestic rate poundage will be 7 or 8 times less than the illustrative figure quoted in Figure B2. The problem is that the impact of revaluation will be uneven both between areas and between different types of business and commercial property. Transitional protection will be provided to limit the combined impact of revaluation and the national non-domestic rate, particularly on small businesses. The only absolute certainty is that confusion will reign for some years.

Government grants

As indicated in Figure B3, the new system will see domestic rate relief grant and block grant replaced by a standard spending grant. The grant entitlement for each local authority area will be calculated to enable all areas to levy the same community charge if they all spend at the level of their needs or standard spending assessments. Grant entitlements for each financial year will be fixed in advance and all grant will be paid into the district or borough collection funds. This means that county councils will not receive standard spending grant, which is a major change from the present system.

The needs assessment will remain a key component of the new grant system but the Government is determined to make it simpler and more stable. This is a seemingly laudable objective until it is realised that the present complexities of GREA are the result of persistent efforts over the last seven or eight years to achieve a fairer outcome. What is particularly worrying is that the Government intends that a comparison between an authority's needs assessment and its actual spending should be a key element of the community charge demand note. In this respect the quest for greater accountability could be seriously flawed.

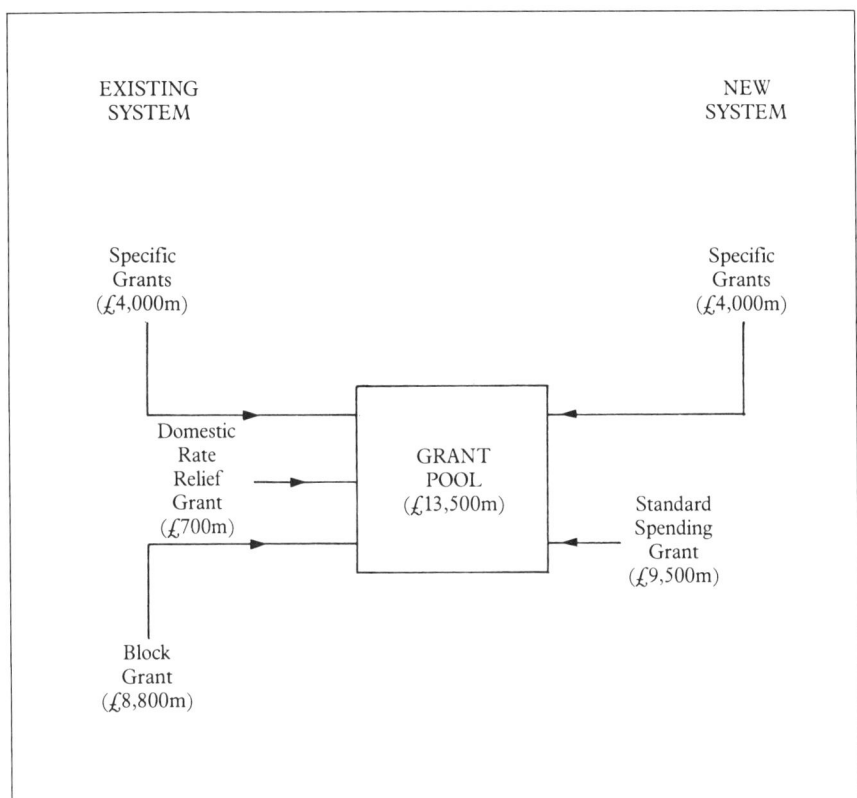

EXISTING
SYSTEM

NEW
SYSTEM

Specific
Grants
(£4,000m)

Specific
Grants
(£4,000m)

Domestic
Rate
Relief
Grant
(£700m)

GRANT
POOL
(£13,500m)

Standard
Spending
Grant
(£9,500m)

Block
Grant
(£8,800m)

Figure B3 – Grant system *England 1989/90*

Community charge

The community charge will bridge the gap between the spending by all local authorities in a particular area and the amounts received in respect of non-domestic rates and standard spending grant. It will take the form of a flat rate tax on all adults and has therefore been described as a poll tax.

As usual there are a number of complications. Firstly, as well as the personal community charge there will be a standard community charge for vacant property and second homes, and a collective community charge for rented and other accommodation in multiple residence where the turnover of residents is high. Secondly, not every adult will be required to pay the full charge. At present the list of total or partial exemptions is as follows:

▽ under-nineteens still at school;
▽ resident National Health Service hospital patients;
▽ persons detained in mental hospitals;
▽ seriously mentally handicapped people;

▽ residents of nursing homes and hostels receiving care;
▽ prisoners (except those in prison for non-payment);
▽ the homeless and persons in night shelters or hostels;
▽ monks and nuns;
▽ community service volunteers;
▽ residents of barracks and certain other Crown buildings;
▽ members of visiting armed forces and their dependants;
▽ diplomats;
▽ full-time students — liable for 20 % only;
▽ people on income support — liable for 20 % only.

Other features of the new system will be the community charge register

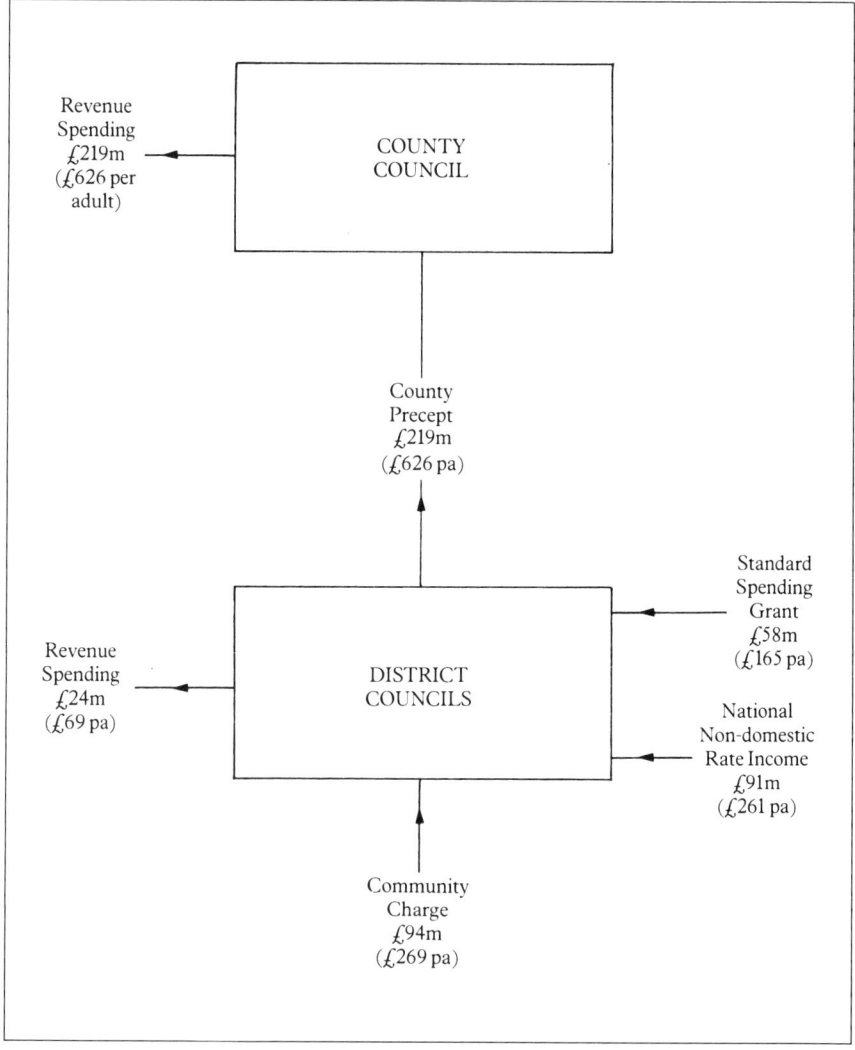

Figure B4 – New system of Local Government Finance

which will be separate from the electoral register and the requirement for every adult to receive a separate bill in a separate envelope, even where two or more adults are resident at the same address.

The impact of the new system is shown in Figure B4 which is in the same format as Figure B1. In cash terms the county precept is much higher than before because no standard spending grant flows direct to the County Council. Perhaps the key point to note is that central funding (standard spending grant plus national non-domestic rate) has increased from £83 million to £149 million. The local tax base (community charge) now represents only 39 % of local authority spending compared with 65 % before. As any increase in local spending has to be met entirely from the community charge, this means that a 1 % increase in local authority spending will cause a 2 % increase in the community charge. This phenomenon is known as gearing and is probably the feature of the new system on which the Government is counting above all to achieve the objective of greater local accountability.

Should this mechanism fail to curb local spending there is still, of course, community charge capping. The combination of the national non-domestic rate and community charge capping will represent an even more formidable array of controls than is currently provided by rate capping. In order to target individual authorities capping will be applied to expenditure levels rather than community charge levels. Another important development is the provision for the Government to apply capping currently rather than retrospectively. Whereas an authority deemed to be over spending in one year is at present rate capped in the following year, the 1988 Act enables the Government to force an authority which has been identified as an overspender in a given year to reduce its spending in that year. This will create even more procedural nightmares for capped authorities than exist at the moment. Although there is no need for non-finance managers to be familiar with the detailed mechanics of community charge capping, it is important to be aware of its existence and potency in case it is brought into play in the years ahead.

Appendix C: The definition and control of capital expenditure

Introduction

Capital expenditure has for some time been one of the most problematic and least satisfactory areas of local government finance. There has been long-standing controversy and confusion about:

(a) definition — how to define capital spending and, in particular, how to achieve a clear distinction between capital and revenue spending;
(b) capital controls — the justification for, and the nature and extent of government controls over capital spending by local authorities;
(c) capital accounting — how best to present capital assets and capital transactions in local authority accounts, and how best to reflect capital asset usage in service costs.

This Appendix will concentrate on issues (a) and (b) on the grounds that issue (c) is not yet fully resolved and, indeed, will merit a volume of its own when it is.

Definition of capital expenditure

Before venturing further it is advisable to review the basic ideas which underpin the separate treatment of capital spending. To the layman there is no intrinsic difference between capital and revenue spending. In either case money is paid out to acquire a commodity or service which will be of use to the organisation. However there is a distinction between capital and revenue spending and it lies in the following characteristics:

∇ the scale of the transaction;
∇ the nature of the commodity or service acquired;
∇ how the money is obtained to pay for the commodity or service, i.e. the method of finance.

Table C1 highlights the difference.

The first criterion is based on practice rather than theory. The scale of a transaction should not determine whether expenditure is capital or revenue. In practice, however, capital expenditure necessitates more record-keeping. Small transactions are often assumed therefore to be 'de minimis' and are treated as revenue expenditure. It is a grave admission for professional accountants to confess to such a pragmatic approach!

Table C1

	Capital spending	Revenue spending
Scale of transaction	Relatively large	Relatively small
Nature of commodity/service	Of long-term value	Consumed immediately or of only short-term value
Method of finance	External loan	Revenue resources
Example	Building a new school	Wages of cleaning staff

As far as the second of these criteria is concerned, the distinction is one of degree. There is no clear boundary which can be applied and this leads to some overlapping in practice. For example, the acquisition of a small piece of land perhaps costing no more than £5,000 would be deemed capital expenditure whereas a £50,000 bill for the consumption of electricity would be a revenue cost. The purchase of a book would always be classified as revenue expenditure even though it could have a longer useful life than a mechanical road sweeper which might well be treated as capital expenditure. If, however, an authority is stocking a new library with a large supply of books, that expenditure might well be classified as capital outlay.

The third criterion, method of finance, is a logical extension of the first two, particularly to non-accountants. If an individual or organisation is contemplating the acquisition of a very costly item, it may simply be a matter of necessity for the transaction to be funded by a loan. Even if there is sufficient money in the bank to meet the entire cost of the acquisition it may well be sensible to take out a loan and thereby spread the cost over a period of years. As well as assisting cash flow in the short term, this will allow the payments profile to be matched against the flow of benefits which the asset will provide. This scenario emphasises the investment nature of most capital spending by corporate organisations, including local authorities.

External borrowing by local authorities is subject to a variety of statutory constraints. One of the most important is that local authorities are not allowed to borrow for revenue purposes (except on a very short-term basis). Any expenditure funded by borrowing will thus be capital expenditure. The reverse is not true however, as many local authorities fund significant amounts of capital spending each year from their revenue budgets. Non-finance managers should be aware therefore that the link between capital expenditure and borrowing is not absolute.

So far we have tried to explain the nature of local authority capital expenditure. However, there remains the need for a rigorous definition and that put forward by the Chartered Institute of Public Finance and Accountancy (CIPFA) in 1983 is probably the most useful. It runs as follows:

> Any outlay which is of value to the authority in the provision of its services beyond the end of the year of account should be recorded as a capital asset provided there is no legal constraint. Capital outlays which are very small in relation to the general magnitude of such outlays may be recorded in an

aggregate minor capital assets account. Capital outlays which are not material to the size and nature of the local authority or which could be consumed in the following accounting period should normally be disregarded in the assets accounts.

The major components of capital expenditure are — acquisition of land and existing buildings; construction and improvement of buildings and civil engineering works, including fees and the cost of the authority's own professional staff connected with those works; acquisition, renewal or replacement of vehicles, vessels, major plant, furniture and equipment and similar items.

These components are not comprehensive and interpretation will differ. Generally, however, ordinary jobbing maintenance to buildings, including painting and decorating should not be defined as capital. Improvement works and significant reconstruction works, such as re-roofing, can be defined as capital. Likewise, significant improvements to, and reconstruction of, roads would be capital expenditure. On no account should any salary or wages other than those directly attributable to the expenditure defined in this schedule be taken as capital expenditure.

The most recent attempt to update this definition can be found in the Local Government and Housing Bill, which applies the 'capital' label to the following categories of expenditure:

▽   the acquisition of land and the acquisition or replacement of buildings, vehicles, plant, machinery and equipment;
▽   the construction of buildings and roads, the installation of plant, machinery and equipment and the enhancement of property;
▽   grants or loans to support capital spending by other persons;
▽   investments (excluding trust funds and temporary deposits).

A new element in this approach is the attempt to distinguish clearly between the enhancement or improvement of property, and repairs and maintenance to property, which has been a persistent 'grey area' in the past. Enhancement is now deemed to include any expenditure which substantially:

▽   lengthens the life of an asset; or
▽   increases its market value; or
▽   extends its existing use.

Such expenditure is within the new definition of capital expenditure. However the new statutory definition does not include repairs and maintenance. Expenditure on repairs and maintenance is therefore a revenue cost. This means that from April 1990:

▽   it cannot be classified as capital expenditure;
▽   it is not subject to capital controls;
▽   it cannot be financed by borrowing.

Confused? — good — so are many accountants, including ourselves.

Capital controls

The existing capital control system has been in place since 1980 although it has been considerably refined in the interim. It seeks to control the amount a local authority spends in any financial year for capital purposes. It has been singularly unsuccessful in achieving most of the Government's stated objectives which are:

▽   to provide the Government with an effective means of influencing local authority capital expenditure and borrowing;
▽   to ensure that the distribution of capital spending reflects both national and local needs;
▽   to encourage asset sales and thereby reduce the size of the public sector;
▽   to enable local authorities to plan capital programmes with reasonable certainty;
▽   to reduce the overall level of local authority debt.

Local authority CFOs are an inventive breed and they have contrived various legal devices which have increased local flexibility at the expense of some of the above objectives. These include advanced purchase schemes, deferred purchase schemes, sale/lease and leaseback arrangements, barter, in-and-out schemes and the cascade principle (see below).

Consequently a new capital control system has been introduced in the Local Government and Housing Bill and will apply from April 1990. The new system is intended to be more simple than its predecessor has become and to shore up the 'deficiencies' in the 1980 system. It is based mainly on controlling what may be borrowed in each financial year, which, incidentally, is how local authority capital spending was controlled prior to 1980.

Financing capital expenditure

If an individual wants to buy a house, he or she must either borrow money from a bank or building society, or persuade a benevolent third party to foot the bill, or use his or her own savings or, more usually, apply the proceeds from selling an existing property to fund the purchase. Any combination of these options is also possible. In exactly the same way, capital spending by a local authority can be financed in four ways:

▽   borrowing or other credit arrangements, such as leasing of property and equipment;
▽   government grants or contributions/donations from third parties;
▽   the authority's own funds and capital resources, e.g. revenue or capital funds, capital receipts (amounts realised from the disposal of surplus capital assets);
▽   the revenue account (i.e. the Community Charge).

Existing system

The existing capital control arrangements apply throughout the 1989/90 financial year. Virtually all capital spending is designated as prescribed expenditure and counts against the Government's annual block spending approvals, irrespective of how it is financed. However, a few categories of expenditure are classified as 'non-prescribed' and do not count against the controls. These are:

▽ de minimis expenditure — individual vehicles and items of equipment costing less than £6,000;
▽ health and safety — expenditure required to bring a building into a fit state for use under health and safety regulations;
▽ operating leases — vehicles and equipment financed by operating leases;

An operating lease is one where:

▽ ownership remains with the lessor, which may be a bank or finance house, and does not pass to the lessee at any stage;
▽ the asset has a residual value of at least 10 % at the end of the lease period;
▽ the residual value does not accrue to the lessee;
▽ renewal or extension of the lease is at not less than the market value.

Apart from the ownership criterion, the possible drawbacks with operating leases are potentially higher cost and excessive administration, since a detailed record of each individual leased item will need to be kept so that it can be returned to the owner (lessor) at the end of the fixed term of the lease.

The existing system has provided limited flexibility between years in allowing a 10 % carry forward from one year to the next. This has been exploited to the full. The only other useful area of flexibility has been the ability to augment capital spending allocations by 20 % of accumulated housing capital receipts and 30 % of accumulated non-housing capital receipts in each financial year. The 'cascade' principle of allowing these percentages to be applied in succeeding years to the reducing balance of the capital receipt has enhanced allocations to a far greater extent than was intended by the Government.

New system

From April 1990, any capital expenditure which is financed by borrowing or other credit arrangements will count against an authority's 'basic credit approval'. This will be fixed by Government before the start of each financial year. It will place an absolute limit on the amount of capital expenditure for that year which can be financed from borrowing. The capital value of any assets acquired through property lease, finance lease and hire/deferred purchase schemes will also count against the limit. However, the limit will not apply to operating leases.

Capital spending which is financed by grants or contributions will be free from control. It must be emphasised that this applies only to contributions or donations from third parties; it does not apply to loans from third parties which do count against the credit approval.

Where the Authority's own resources are used, the relevant capital expenditure will also not count against the credit approval. This applies to revenue contributions as well as to the use of internal funds. However, only 50 % of capital receipts will be available to finance new capital spending. This is more restrictive than the 20 or 30 % limit under the present control system because it will no longer be possible to use the 'cascade' approach. The other

50 % will have to be used to repay the debt outstanding on previous borrowing. It is also important to understand precisely what is meant by 'financing from revenue'; for such expenditure to be free from control it must be charged in full to the revenue account in the year during which it is incurred. At the corporate level the use of direct revenue financing will be limited by the impact it will have on the community charge. This again introduces the issue of accountability. Unless its community charge is capped, a local authority will no longer be able to plead that central government is preventing it from incurring capital expenditure. The authority's capital programme will be limited only by the willingness of its community charge payers to meet the bill.

Just how the new system will work will not become clear until the Local Government and Housing Bill completes its passage through Parliament and the detailed regulations which are required to amplify the basic legislation are issued. One fundamental weakness of the existing system will clearly remain, namely the annual nature of capital controls. Whatever the justification for Government control over local authority capital spending it is surely fair to argue that the planning of capital investment requires some reasonable idea of future prospects in the medium and long term. For this exercise to be at the mercy of an annual rationing process which, based on past experience, is neither stable nor predictable must surely remain one of the more bizarre characteristics of local government finance.

Appendix D: Service level agreements

The aim of this Appendix is to summarise very briefly some of the issues which need to be covered in drawing up and implementing service level agreements (SLAs) between the CFO's department and service departments. To supplement this an extract from a provisional SLA which we are discussing within our own authority is attached. The extract comprises the covering document plus an Appendix dealing with the creditor payments function. SLAs for other functions have also been prepared.

The principal matters that must be covered in the SLA are:

(a) the period of the agreement;
(b) the scope of the agreement — the broad functions which it covers, e.g. payroll, creditor payments, income, financial advice, internal audit;
(c) the detailed terms and conditions under which each function will be performed (see below);
(d) the basis on which charges will be calculated and levied (see below);
(e) arrangements for extension or renewal of the agreement;
(f) monitoring arrangements;
(g) arbitration procedures in the event of a dispute;
(h) procedures and penalties in the event of poor performance or default;

The terms and conditions referred to at (c) above will have three principal components:

▽ A detailed specification of the services to be provided by the CFO's department.
▽ A list of requirements that must be met, and by whom, so that the CFO can fulfil his or her statutory responsibility (see chapter 2); these are described as 'minimum requirements'. They need not be part of the SLA itself and might instead be appended to financial regulations or form a separate supporting manual of financial instructions.
▽ Details of any performance standards that will apply.

There are various bases on which charges can be calculated. These include:

▽ A fixed fee: A single fee could cover all functions performed by the CFO's department or separate fees could be agreed for each function.
▽ A banded charge: This is an extension of the fixed fee whereby the fee increases in discrete steps according to the workload on a particular

function. There would need to be a separate scale of charges for each function.

▽ Unit charges: Unit charges such as £x per payroll employee or y pence per creditor invoice could be agreed. Such unit charges might be based either on:

— Average cost — the total cost of carrying out the function, including fixed costs, divided by the number of units.

— Marginal cost — the variable cost per unit or the additional cost which would be incurred if the workload increased by one unit.

If a marginal cost basis were used to set the unit charges there would need to be a lump sum fee as well to cover fixed costs.

It may be appropriate for the statement of charges to include a mechanism for dealing with inflation. Numerous alternatives are available; our preference would be to increase charges in line with the July pay award for administrative, professional and clerical staff. The alternative would be a cash-limit approach whereby charges were fixed for a given future period (say one year). Provision would then have to be made for periodic reviews.

Considerable care needs to be taken in setting up the framework of charges. In particular account should be taken of:

▽ Risk — the greater the fixed element of any charge, the fewer the problems caused to the CFO's department by reductions in service activity. However, the converse also applies and a high fixed fee element is vulnerable to higher than expected increases in work volumes.

▽ Incentives — unit charges which reflect the differences in resource input to each process can be a means of encouraging the client department to limit their demand for processes which impose high costs on the CFO's department, e.g. submitting invoices for urgent payment.

▽ Data requirements — the more sophisticated the charging basis used, the greater the volume of data which are likely to be required to calculate the charges. This could impose a significant burden on the CFO's staff in collecting and recording the data, and on staff in the client department who have to monitor and verify the charges.

Annex to Appendix D

Service Level Agreement
XXXXX Department

1.0   Introduction

1.1   This agreement covers the services that the County Treasurer provides to the xxxxx Department to ensure the efficient and economic discharge of its financial commitments.

1.2   The main functions covered are payrolls, creditor payments, income collection, accountancy, internal audit, insurances and financial advice/consultancy.

2.0   Minimum requirements

2.1   To meet his statutory obligations under the Local Government Act 1972 and Local Government Finance Act 1988, the County Treasurer requires certain minimum standards and controls to apply to the financial transactions of the xxxxx Department. These are designed to ensure that the following objectives are met:

Activity/function	Objective
Payrolls	To effect accurately all and only valid payroll transactions on the due dates.
Creditor payments	To discharge correctly and promptly all liabilities to creditors.
Income collection	To collect and bank promptly all income due.
Accountancy/audit/ financial advice	To assist the client department in preparing its revenue and capital plans and to record its transactions so that necessary accounts, returns and measures of financial performance can be provided.

2.2   The detailed minimum standards and controls for each activity/ function are set out in the relevant enclosures to this agreement. These minimum requirements cannot be amended without the prior agreement of the County Treasurer but, in the interests of efficiency, they will be reviewed periodically or as circumstances demand.

3.0   Documentation and training

3.1   The County Treasurer's Department will provide user manuals for each function covered by this agreement, together with up to xx days per annum of training for xxxxx Department staff.

3.2   If the County Treasurer or the Service Chief Officer deem further training to be needed, this will be provided by the County Treasurer's Department for an additional fee (to be negotiated at that time).

4.0   Facilities provided and timescales

4.1   The facilities to be provided on each function by the County
        Treasurer, and the timescales involved, are set out in the relevant
        enclosures to this agreement:

Payrolls   — Enclosure 1
Creditors payments   — Enclosure 2
Income collection   — Enclosure 3
Accountancy/audit/financial advice   — Enclosure 4

5.0   Charges

5.1   The charges for the provision of these services will include both a
        fixed fee and unit charges. The fixed annual fee will be £z'000. In
        addition, there will be a unit charge for each function, as set out in
        Enclosures 1 to 4 of this agreement.
5.2   Both the fixed fee and the unit charges will be subject to review at
        intervals of not less than one year. Proposed variations will be notified
        in writing at least x months in advance of the date from which they are
        intended to apply.

6.0   Variations/arbitration

6.1   The terms and conditions of this agreement may be reviewed if either
        party requests major changes in the specification after the operative
        date, provided that both parties agree to a review.
6.2   Every effort should be made to settle disputes without recourse to a
        third party. Where such efforts fail, the County Solicitor will
        arbitrate. If the County Solicitor's decision is unacceptable to either
        party, the Performance Review and Special Purposes Sub-committee
        will act as the final arbiter.

7.0   Penalties

7.1   In the event of any financial loss which arises as a result of error it will
        be open to either Department to use the procedure in paragraph 6.2
        above if it considers compensation to be appropriate.

8.0   Periods of agreement and notice

8.1   This agreement will be for a period of xx months, ending on xxxxxxx.
8.2   Amendment or premature termination of the agreement will be
        subject to xx months' notice in writing.

_____ xxxxx Department Authorisation
_____ Treasurer's Department Agreement
_____ Date of Agreement

Service Level Agreement
XXXXX Department

CREDITOR PAYMENTS

1   Purpose of Enclosure

1.1   This enclosure sets out the minimum requirements, facilities provided, timescales and unit charges referred to in paragraphs 2.2, 4.1 and 5.1 of the Service Level Agreement between the County Treasurer and XXXXX Department dated XXXX.

2   Minimum Requirements

Responsibility of:

2.1	Standing Orders and Financial Regulations must be observed at all times.	CT/Service
2.2	All statutory requirements must be complied with.	CT/Service
2.3	Ordering of goods or services must be in accordance with financial regulations.	Service
2.4	The duties of ordering, receiving and paying for goods or services must be undertaken by separate individuals unless otherwise agreed with the County Treasurer.	Service
2.5	Correct accounting codes must be entered on all vouchers.	Service
2.6	All vouchers submitted for payment must be certified by an officer approved for this purpose by the County Treasurer and Service Chief Officer.	Service
2.7	Certification signatures must be checked selectively against specimen signatures, for authenticity.	CT
2.8	All invoices or copies thereof must be stored to comply with statutory requirements or agreements.	CT/Service
2.9	Cheque details must be checked before despatch.	CT
2.10	All entries to the accounting ledgers must be checked for accuracy and completeness.	CT/Service
2.11	A bank reconciliation must be carried out.	CT
2.12	Integrity of computer programmes and data must be maintained.	CT
2.13	An audit trail must be maintained.	CT/Service
2.14	Creditor payment procedures must be reviewed annually by Internal Audit.	CT/Service

3   Facilities provided by the County Treasurer

3.1   Supply the system stationery.

3.2   Supply the user manual and train staff.

3.3   Separate urgent and non-urgent invoices when received from the XXXXX Department.

3.4   Check the certification signature on selected invoices against specimen signatures.

3.5   Enter creditor and remittance details on system stationery/invoice coding slip.

3.6   Set up computerised 'creditor details' record for all new creditors.
3.7   Test check invoices to confirm that certification checks have been properly applied.
3.8   Enter tracer number on all invoices to provide an audit trail.
3.9   Identify invoices from sub-contractors, confirm that these comply with current regulations, and pursue with the sub-contractor any that do not.
3.10   Prepare cheques to creditors and confirm details against invoice details.
3.11   Despatch cheques to creditors.
3.12   Enter payment details in creditors' ledger and general ledger.
3.13   File and store all invoices or copies thereof in accordance with current legislation/agreements.
3.14   Reclaim any VAT from H.M. Customs and Excise.
3.15   Carry out bank reconciliation of all creditor payments.
3.16   Deal with any queries received from creditors, XXXXX Department staff and HM Customs and Excise Officers.
3.17   Monitor/advise the XXXXX Department to ensure compliance with statutory requirements.

4   Timescales

4.1   Invoices may be submitted to the Treasurer's Department on any working day, but attempts should be made to even out the workload wherever possible.
4.2   Invoices marked 'urgent' will be paid within X working days of receipt by the Treasurer's Department.
4.3   Invoices not marked as urgent will be paid within XX working days of receipt by the Treasurer's Department.
4.4   In exceptional circumstances, invoices can be paid on the day of receipt by the Treasurer's Department but these "emergency" procedures must be strictly limited.

5   Unit charges

5.1   The following charges will apply per invoice processed:

Type of Invoice	Charge per Invoice (pence)
Non-urgent	x
Urgent	y
Emergency	z

5.2   Incorrectly completed invoices may be referred back to the XXXX Department for correction. Such invoices will be charged as processed by the Treasurer's Department at the time of referral and their resubmission will result in a further unit charge for processing.

Glossary of financial terms

Most of this glossary is reproduced from the Local Authority Finance Glossary published by the Chartered Institute of Public Finance and Accountancy.

Accounts: a generic term for statements setting out details of income and expenditure over an accounting period (usually a year) or assets and liabilities at the end of the period, or both, in a structured manner

Aggregate exchequer grant (AEG): the total amount of government grant made available each year to local government, which is expressed as a percentage of approved relevant expenditure

Aggregate external finance (AEF): the total of central support for local authorities' revenue expenditure from April 1990 when the new system of local government finance is introduced. It will comprise government grants and income from the uniform national non-domestic rate

Appropriation: the transfer of ownership of land or a building that is no longer required by one local authority service to another

Asset: something of worth which is measurable in monetary terms, e.g. land, buildings, equipment, goodwill.

Asset rent: an annual charge to the user of a fixed asset, based on a suitable valuation of that asset

Audit: an independent examination of an organisation's activities, either by internal audit or the organisation's external auditor

Audit commission: an independent body created by the Local Government Finance Act 1982 with responsibility for the external audit of all local authority accounts from 1st April 1983

Auditor's opinion: the opinion that is required by statute from an authority's external auditors, indicating whether the audit has been completed in accordance with Part III of the Local Government Act 1982, the Code of Audit Practice and whether the statement of accounts presents fairly the financial position of the authority

Balance sheet: a statement of the recorded assets and liabilities at a specific date at the end of an accounting period

Balances: the capital or revenue reserves of an authority made up of the accumulated surplus of income over expenditure on the general rate fund, county fund, community charge collection fund or any other fund

Block grant: the major element of rate support grant established under the Local Government Planning and Land Act 1980. The main form of central government aid towards the cost of local authority services in general. To be replaced by revenue support grant (standard spending grant) from April 1990

Budget: a statement of an authority's forecast of net revenue and capital expenditure over a specified period of time

Budget head: each section of the budget for which estimates are produced and control exercised

Business plan: a plan covering a specified future period (usually more than one year) which sets out an organisation's objectives, forecasts and resource requirements, and may also include targets or performance standards against which achievements can be measured

Capital accounts: the accounts which record all transactions relating to capital expenditure and income, i.e. capital receipts. Local authorities keep these accounts on the basis of receipts and payments made in the accounting period

Capital allocations: the main method by which capital expenditure is at present controlled by central government. The allocations are annual amounts specified by government and they substantially determine the maximum capital payments which a local authority may make in that year (see 'capital controls')

Capital controls: the various methods by which the level of capital expenditure is controlled by central government

Capital employed: the assets used by an organisation to undertake its activities

Capital expenditure: expenditure on the acquisition of significant fixed assets which will be of use or benefit to an authority in

providing its services beyond the year of account

Capital financing: the raising of money to pay for capital expenditure. It covers borrowing, leasing, revenue contributions to capital outlay, capital receipts, capital grants, capital fund and other contributions

Capital fund: an internal reserve to finance capital expenditure without resort to external borrowing

Capital programme: the capital projects an authority proposes to undertake over a stated period of time

Capital receipt: proceeds from the sale of a fixed asset e.g. land or a building. Capital receipts can be used to repay debt or to finance new capital expenditure

Cash limit: a method of expenditure control which restricts the amount available for spending for a particular purpose to a specified amount, regardless of the effects of inflation

Central establishment charges: see support services

Collecting authority: a borough or district council with the statutory responsibility to administer a community charge collection fund and to appoint a community charge collection officer

Commitment accounting: a system whereby transactions are recorded at the time the commitment arises. Commitments are initially recorded when orders are issued or received and are deleted when invoices are paid or money received at which time the transaction will be recorded in the traditional way

Committed expenditure: expenditure in respect of goods, services and works for which orders have been placed or tenders accepted but for which payment has not been made

Community charge: the local tax which will replace domestic rates in April 1990. It will bridge the gap between the spending by all local authorities in a particular area and the amounts received in respect of non-domestic rates and revenue support grant. It will take the form of a flat rate tax on all adults, and is also known as the poll tax

Continuation budget: the cost of existing policies and standards of service provision in a future year, before developments or reductions, expressed at a specified price base

Core function: a financial management function which is retained under the direct control of the CFO either to enable his or her statutory role as responsible financial officer to be fulfilled, or on the grounds of efficiency

Cost centre: the term for each individual unit to which items of income and expenditure are charged for either managerial or detailed control purposes, e.g. a vehicle or school

County fund: the main fund of a county council into which all receipts are paid from which all and liabilities are met, and which summarises the cost of most of the services provided by the authority (see also 'general rate fund')

Credit approval: a statutory limit on the annual amount of capital expenditure by a local authority which can be financed by borrowing or other credit arrangements. This borrowing control will replace the existing control on spending from April 1990

Creditor: an amount owed for work done, goods received, or services rendered before the end of the

accounting period, but for which payment has not been made by the end of that accounting period

Current asset: an asset where the value may change because the volume held can vary through day-to-day activity, e.g. physical stockholdings

Current expenditure: the direct revenue costs of local authority service provision; it excludes indirect costs such as capital financing costs

Current liability: an amount which will become payable or could be called in within the next accounting period. e.g. creditor, cash overdrawn. (See 'liability')

Debt charges: annual charges to the revenue accounts of local authority services to cover the interest on, and repayment of, loans for capital expenditure; a major component of capital financing costs

Debt outstanding: amounts borrowed principally to finance capital expenditure or working capital which are still to be repaid

Debtor: an amount due for work done, goods provided or services rendered, receivable by the end of the accounting period, but for which reimbursement has not, at that time, been received

Depreciation: the theoretical loss in value of an asset due to age, wear and tear, deterioration, or obsolescence. Depreciation is charged to profit and loss, trading or revenue accounts to reflect asset usage

Direct service organisation (DSO): an organisation which consists of people directly employed by an authority (including supervisory and support staff, and their accommodation, equipment, etc.) to carry out work which is subject to compulsory competitive tendering

Domestic rate relief grant: a government grant paid to a rating authority to compensate for the statutory reduction in the rate levy paid by domestic ratepayers. It will be discontinued when domestic rates are replaced by the community charge in April 1990

Estimates: the forecasts of expenditure and income for an accounting period (see 'budget')

Expenditure determination: an expenditure assessment determined by the Secretary of State for the Environment in respect of each authority designated for rate or precept limitation under the Rates Act 1984. It is used to derive the maximum rate or precept which the authority is permitted to levy. The process is known as rate capping

Financial regulations: a written code agreed by an authority to provide a framework within which to conduct its financial affairs. The regulations govern the procedures to be followed by all managers in relation to financial functions and they are intended to ensure financial integrity (probity)

Fixed asset: an asset which has value beyond one financial year

Fixed cost: a cost which does not directly vary with the volume of service or the number of units produced, e.g. plant and premises costs will not usually vary in the short term

General rate fund (GRF): the main fund of a rating authority into which all receipts are paid and from which all liabilities are met, and which summarises the cost of most of the services provided by the authority

Grant limitation: the procedure by which an authority's block grant gains or losses in moving from one financial year to the next are limited. Limitation of grant or other losses is usually referred to as safety netting

Grant related expenditure assessment (GREA): an assessment by government of how much each individual local authority would have to spend to provide a common level of service; to be replaced by the needs assessment (standard spending assessment) from April 1990

Gross expenditure: the cost of providing services before the deduction of government grants or other income

Hereditament: a unit of property capable of separate occupation which would be shown as a separate item on the valuation lists for rating purposes

Historic cost: amounts recorded at their original cost, and not adjusted for the effect of subsequent price changes

Housing benefits: a national system of financial assistance to individuals towards certain housing costs, which is administered by local authorities on behalf of central government. Assistance takes the form of rate rebates, rent rebates and rent allowances. From April 1990 rate rebates will be replaced by community charge rebates

Housing revenue account (HRA): an account which includes the expenditure and income arising in connection with the provision of housing accommodation by a local authority

Housing subsidy: government grant payable to housing authorities towards the cost of the provision of local authority housing and its management and maintenance

Improvement grants: statutory or discretionary payments that local authorities make to tenants or home-owners to provide basic amenities and enable them to bring dwellings up to modern standards

Inflation provision: an allowance within a budget which is designed to cover variations in costs of providing services from the price base at which the budget was prepared to the end of the accounting period

Insurance fund: an internal reserve created to provide finance to make good, in whole or in part, loss or damage suffered by the authority

Interest: an amount received or paid for the use of a sum of money when it is invested or borrowed

Joint board: a legally separate body with a power to levy a precept, comprising representatives of two or more local authorities. Joint boards exist in the metropolitan areas and London to provide certain services which were administered by metropolitan county councils or the Greater London Council prior to their abolition, e.g. the fire service

Joint finance: capital or revenue finance available from health authorities for the use of local authorities to provide certain specified services. May be 100 %, for example on capital projects, or a percentage often tapering to nil after a number of years

Leasing: a method of financing capital expenditure where a rental charge is paid for an asset for a specified period of time

Liability: an amount due to an individual or organisation which will be paid at some time in the future. Liabilities include debt outstanding and creditors

Loans fund: a fund into which borrowed monies are paid and from which advances are made to individual capital accounts to finance capital expenditure instead of raising earmarked loans for each individual item

Loans outstanding: the total amounts borrowed from external lenders for capital and temporary revenue purposes but not repaid at the balance sheet date

Management accounting: the provision of information, particularly costing information, primarily to aid decision-making

Minimum standards: the minimum levels of control, e.g. authorisations, checks, required by the CFO, as responsible financial officer, to be applied to each non-core financial management function to ensure financial integrity (probity)

Needs assessment: the new term to describe the grant-related expenditure assessment. It is the amount of revenue expenditure, net of specific grants, which it is appropriate for each authority to incur in providing a common standard of service. It is also known as the standard spending assessment

Net assets: the total assets of an organisation less its liabilities

Net expenditure: the cost of providing a service after the deduction of specific grants and other sources of income but excluding block grant or standard spending grant and rate income

Out-turn: the actual expenditure and income for a particular year of account, or other accounting period

Out-turn prices: the actual level of prices encountered during an accounting period

Overheads: expenses not directly allocated to a cost centre but apportioned by way of an agreed procedure

Penny rate product: the amount which would be raised by an authority levying a rate or precept of one penny in the pound on the rateable value of the authority's area, after allowing for losses on rate collection and for certain costs of collection

Pooling: a means of redistributing certain expenditure which otherwise would fall disproportionately on a limited number of local authorities

Precept: a statutory demand by which a non-rating authority obtains the income it requires via the appropriate rating authorities to meet its net expenditure requirements

Prescribed expenditure: the capital expenditure of local authorities, as defined by government for the purposes of its existing capital expenditure controls. The term will no longer be relevant when the new system of capital controls, based on borrowing, is introduced in April 1990

Price base: the levels of the rates of pay and prices of goods and services at a specified date

Public expenditure: the combined spending of central and local government together with government loans and grants to public corporations and the nationalised industries

Public Works Loan Board (PWLB): a government agency which provides long-term loans to local authorities at interest rates only slightly higher than those at which the government itself can borrow

Rateable value: the annual assumed rental value of a hereditament

Rate capping: the term applied to the provisions of the Rates Act 1984, by which government may set rate or precept limits for specific authorities. From April 1990 it will be succeeded by community charge capping under the terms of the Local Government Finance Act 1988

Rate levy: the number of pence in the pound that a rating authority decides should be applied to the rateable value of each of the hereditaments in its area to determine the rate payable by their occupiers to finance precepts and its net expenditure

Rate of return — DSO: for each direct service organisation an authority operates, the government sets a target rate of return, usually expressed as a percentage of capital employed. Failure to achieve its target rate of return for three successive years may result in a government directive to wind up the DSO

Rate rebate: a reduction in the liability to rates of any specific domestic rate-payer (as opposed to the general reduction of domestic rate relief) granted in accordance with a national means test

Rate support grant: a general grant paid by government to local authorities to help them finance the cost of their services. To be replaced by revenue support grant (standard spending grant) from April 1990

Rating authority: an authority which levies a rate to finance both its own expenditure and that of other authorities which precept on it

Real terms spending: a level of spending over a period of time, measured on a constant price basis (namely after eliminating the effects of inflation over the period concerned)

Recharge: the transfer of costs from one account to another

Recoupment: the inter-authority charges which arise when one local authority educates pupils or students who are the responsibility of another

Relevant expenditure: the total of all rate-borne expenditure of each local authority ranking for rate or revenue support grant purposes, including spending financed by supplementary and specific grants, e.g. police grant. This may be applied nationally or to a specific authority

Rent allowance: a subsidy payable by a local authority to a low income tenant or sub-tenant in private rented accommodation

Rent rebate: a subsidy payable by a local authority to low income tenants in local authority accommodation

Repairs and renewal fund: a fund an authority can establish to meet the cost of repairing, maintaining, replacing and renewing its buildings, vehicles, plant and equipment

Reserve: amounts included in one period's accounts when the goods or services have been supplied/ received but the actual receipt/ payment occurs in a future accounting period

Revenue account: an account that records an authority's day-to-day expenditure and income on such items as salaries and wages, running costs of services, and the financing costs of capital expenditure

Revenue contribution to capital outlay (RCCO): a charge to the revenue account to finance capital expenditure

Revenue expenditure: the day-to-day costs an authority incurs in providing services

Revenue support grant: see 'standard spending grant'

Revised estimates: the approved estimates for the current year, as updated during that year

Running expenses: the day-to-day running costs an authority incurs in providing services, but specifically excluding direct employee expenses, capital financing costs and revenue contributions to capital outlay

Safety net: a device introduced into the block grant system to limit grant losses or gains from one year to the next

Service level agreement: a written agreement setting out the terms and conditions under which one organisation or department provides services to another

Sinking fund: a fund created for the redemption of a liability or with the object of replacing an asset by setting aside a sum periodically and investing it so as to produce the required amount at the appropriate time

Specific grants: government grants to local authorities in aid of particular projects or services

Standard spending assessment: see 'needs assessment'

Standard spending grant: the replacement for rate support grant under the new system of local government finance to be introduced in April 1990. Standard spending grant is paid only in support of expenditure up to the level of the needs or standard spending assessment

Standing orders : formal rules an authority draws up to regulate its proceedings and the conduct of its business

Statement of accounts: the published accounts of an authority on which the external auditor gives an opinion. Under the Local Government Finance Act 1982, authorities are required to publish their statements of accounts within nine months of the end of each financial year

Subjective analysis: the classification of expenditure and income according to the nature of the items, e.g. salaries, fuel, telephones

Superannuation fund: a fund comprising sums deducted from employees' pay and employers' contributions, from which a range of pension benefits is paid to contributors, their widows and, where appropriate, dependent children

Supplementary estimate: an increase to a budget head during a year, approved in accordance with an authority's financial regulations

Supplementary grants: grants paid by government to authorities on the basis of approved eligible expenditure on particular services, e.g. national parks

Support services: support services are back-up activities of a professional, technical and administrative nature, which are not local authority services in their own right, but give technical, organisational and administrative support to those services

Suspense account: an account which is used for receipts or payments that cannot immediately be allocated because of inadequate information

Temporary loan: money borrowed for an initial period of less than one year

Trust funds: assets owned by an individual or organisation and administered by an authority on their behalf

Value for money: An expression describing the benefit obtained for a given input of resources (not just in financial terms)

Variable costs: a cost which varies directly with the volume of service or the number of units produced, e.g. food costs

Virement: the transfer of a planned expenditure or underspending on one budget head to finance additional spending on another budget head, in accordance with an authority's financial regulations

Working capital: the sums available to meet the day-to-day expenses. Working capital is usually calculated as current assets less current liabilities

Work in progress: the cost of work done on an uncompleted project at a specified date so far as it has not been recharged or recovered at that date

Index